TABLE OF CO[NTENTS]

Contributors

JOHNATHON BOWERS is Instructor of Theology and Christian Worldview at Bethlehem College & Seminary in Minneapolis. In 2015, he began a PhD program in Christian Philosophy at The Southern Baptist Theological Seminary. He lives in Minneapolis with his wife, Crystal, and their son, Charlie.

RYAN GRIFFITH is Assistant Professor of Christian Worldview and Director of the Integrated Curriculum at Bethlehem College & Seminary in Minneapolis, where he teaches biblical studies, church history, and literature. He is also a PhD student at The Southern Baptist Theological Seminary.

DAVID MATHIS is executive editor at desiringGod.org, pastor for Cities Church, Minneapolis, and adjunct professor at Bethlehem College & Seminary. He is co-editor of *Acting the Miracle: God's Work and Ours in the Mystery of Sanctification* and co-author of *How to Stay Christian in Seminary*. He and his wife Megan have three children.

JASON MEYER (PhD, The Southern Baptist Theological Seminary) is pastor for preaching and vision at Bethlehem Baptist Church and associate professor of New Testament at Bethlehem College & Seminary. Prior to coming to Bethlehem, he served as Dean of Chapel and Assistant Professor of Christian Studies at Louisiana College. He is the author of *Preaching: A Biblical Theology* and *The End of the Law: Mosaic Covenant in Pauline Theology*.

Jonathan Parnell is a writer and content strategist at desiring-God.org, and is the lead pastor of Cities Church in Minneapolis–Saint Paul, where he lives with his wife, Melissa, and their five children. He is also the coauthor of *How to Stay Christian in Seminary* (2014).

JOHN PIPER is founder and teacher for desiringGod.org and Chancellor of Bethlehem College & Seminary, Minneapolis. For more than 30 years, he served as pastor at Bethlehem Baptist Church. He is the author of more than 50 books, including *Desiring God: Meditations of a Christian Hedonist* and *Battling Unbelief: Defeating Sin with Superior Pleasure*. More than 30 years of his preaching and teaching ministry is available at desiringGod.org. John and his wife, Noel, have four sons, one daughter, and twelve grandchildren.

TONY REINKE is a content strategist and staff writer for desiringGod.org and the author of *Lit! A Christian Guide to Reading Books* (2011) and *John Newton on the Christian Life: To Live Is Christ* (2015). He hosts the podcast *Ask Pastor John*, and lives in the Twin Cities with his wife and their three children.

JOE RIGNEY is Assistant Professor of Theology and Christian Worldview at Bethlehem College & Seminary, and the author of *The Things of Earth: Treasuring God by Enjoying His Gifts* (2014) and *Live Like a Narnian: Christian Discipleship in Lewis's Chronicles* (2013). He lives in Minneapolis with his wife and two sons.

MARSHALL SEGAL is the executive assistant to John Piper and a writer for desiringGod.org. He is a graduate of Wake Forest University and Bethlehem College & Seminary. He lives in Minneapolis and is a member of Bethlehem Baptist Church.

Introduction

MARSHALL SEGAL

His wife was gone. Sure, last night looked like a lot of nights recently. She'd walked out many times before, but this was different. The abandonment, the adultery, and the deception had mounted a massive assault on their marriage and family. Had it been three men in just six months? He feared there were more. Again and again, she'd wrecked the family's affairs with her own. She had spent and overspent the family budget to please another guy—another illicit, irrational, imaginary love.

Their marriage, once sweet, had become a nightmare. Those first days, maybe even months, of marital bliss felt so distant and unfamiliar. It was hard for her husband to believe they were ever even real. Two children—a son and a daughter—were the real victims, loved by dad, but left by mom. They were conceived and raised in despair and misery. Their dad had always hoped things would change. He even promised that things would be different, that the loneliness and betrayal they'd known their whole lives would be turned for good—for hope, belonging, and love.

Not knowing what to say to his confused and wounded children that night, dad knelt down between their beds, and he prayed:

> *God, please rescue my bride—the mother of my precious children—from this destructive, suicidal path. She's left us for other lovers, believing that with them she'll find the protection and affection she craves. For as long as she runs from the promises we made and the family*

we've built together, graciously cause her to be unsatis-
fied, empty, and lonely. Maybe then, in her despair and
need, she will remember us, return to our family, and be
Wife and Mom again. If she would only come home, I
would welcome her into my arms and heart as if it were
our wedding day. I would love her as if we never lost
her. Bring her home, for the sake of your Name, Amen.
(Hosea 2:5–7)

Several years later, on a hot afternoon in August, the husband
was walking downtown through a local park. His oldest, a
teenager now, had left an assignment on the kitchen table, so
he was dropping it off at school. He could walk from his of-
fice, and usually even enjoyed the break and exercise, but it
was uncomfortable today. Temperatures had soared to record
highs, leaving most people hiding inside until evening. He
saw a woman, though—the only soul he'd seen since he left
work. She was exhausted, disheveled, and desperate. She was
squeezing every last drop out of a public drinking fountain,
clinging to it like she might drown if she let go. As he walked
closer, he started to make out her face.

"Hannah? . . . is that you?" He looked into her eyes and
saw the face he knew so well, the woman who had hurt him
so deeply. She was still his wife. She looked around uncom-
fortably, as if she was waiting for someone else to walk by and
discover her shame. She had left so much for so very little. She
left the provision, safety, and intimacy of a truly good man for
a treadmill of temporary pleasure and terrible, destructive life
choices. The other men always seemed so attractive, but they
never truly loved her, and the relationships never lasted.

"Why are you out here, Hannah?"

"I have nowhere else to go, and I had to get away from
him. . . . I'm tired, and scared, and thirsty."

"Come home, Hannah. You know I will take care of you—whatever you need. I'll provide for you and protect you. You'll never be thirsty again."

After several hard, awkward, silent moments, she finally looked back up at him, feeling lost, embarrassed, and ashamed. He was smiling. It wasn't the cute, naïve, playful smile she saw on their first dates together. No, it had been replaced with something deeper, more refined, and durable. "I love you," he said. She couldn't believe what she was seeing, what she was *hearing*.

"But you don't know what I've done. . . where I've been."

"No, I do. I know about the men. I know about the one at your apartment right now, and the six that came before him. I know each of their names, Hannah. Come home."

"No, you don't understand. I'm not worthy of you anymore."

"Hannah, I never loved you because you were worthy. I loved you because you were mine. And even though you ran away and gave yourself to other men, 'I will betroth you to me in righteousness and in justice.' Even though you walked away from our love and our family, 'I will betroth you to me in steadfast love and in mercy.' Even though you defiled our covenant and failed to fulfill your promises, 'I will betroth you to me in faithfulness.'"

MANKIND'S SEVEN MISTRESSES

". . . And you shall know me, the Lord" (Hosea 2:19–20). We are Hannah, each one of us. The names of our seven affairs are Pride, Envy, Anger, Sloth, Greed, Gluttony, and Lust. And the betrayed, but faithful husband is Jesus—our first love, our lost love, our new love.

Undoubtedly there are sins besides these or other ways for naming them, but the seven deadly sins have been some of the most promiscuous and prevalent in history. They form a brothel of mistresses who are all at once familiar and unfamiliar. They're familiar because every man or woman has tasted them—either for a one-night stand or in a life-long affair. They've seduced the sinful in every culture on every continent through every generation. But somehow they're also unfamiliar. Very few have looked closely enough at their faces to be able to spot them in a crowd or to study the havoc they wreak. They disguise themselves, creep into seemingly harmless situations and conversations, embed themselves deep in our love and devotion, and then giggle when everything begins to unravel and explode. They are the cruelest and most dangerous Bond girls, each beautiful and breathing her own set of lies—outrageous lies and yet they're strangely sweet and compelling.

Pride puts herself above God. She foolishly and suicidally contends for supremacy with God, opposing him and inviting his wrath. Envy can't help being unhappy at the blessing and fortune of others. She seethes as others succeed, and even secretly smiles when they fail. Unrighteous Anger viciously attempts to protect a flawed love. She explodes over selfish, irrelevant things, and carelessly overlooks the things that offend and dishonor God. Sloth desperately attempts to control life in order to preserve her comforts, dreading being interrupted by the needs of others. She is lazy-souled—bored with God and doomed to a slow death. Greed overwhelms her victim with an inordinate desire for wealth and possessions. She covets what she shouldn't or too desperately and impatiently wants what she should. Gluttony looks to food to satisfy some deeper craving, whether for comfort, purpose, or control. She worships food. Lust is a sexual desire that dishonors its object and disregards God. She irrationally seizes sex for selfish gain, believing its pleasure will fill the emptiness she feels.

For as long as we can remember, our souls have been exposed to and enticed by seductive, scantily-clad images of all seven of these women. They've schemed and lied and pled for our affections, and they've too often won the day, or at least the moment. But those who have believed in Jesus have been redeemed from their flirtation and infidelity with sin. We are no longer characterized by or enslaved to our former, illicit lovers. We're forever loved, pursued, provided for, and freed by a deeper, stronger, and truer Love—a lover larger than our past, stronger than our weakness, and better than any we've ever known before.

Jesus once brought this same good news to a woman drawing from a different drinking fountain. He said to that six-man woman, who was stuck in patterns of sin and self-destructive behavior, "Everyone who drinks of this water will be thirsty again, but whoever drinks of the water that I will give him will never be thirsty again. The water that I will give him will become in him a spring of water welling up to eternal life" (John 4:13–14). Jesus came to a spiritual third-world of dry mouths and empty stomachs, and he invited us to come, eat, drink, and live.

> "Come, everyone who thirsts, come to the waters; and he who has no money, come, buy and eat! Come, buy wine and milk without money and without price. Why do you spend your money for that which is not bread, and your labor for that which does not satisfy? Listen diligently to me, and eat what is good, and delight yourselves in rich food. Incline your ear, and come to me; hear, that your soul may live." (Isa. 55:1–3)

Jesus went on to say to the woman at the well—the ashamed, rejected, and ostracized—"The Father is seeking people to worship him" (John 4:23). Not perfect, attractive, deserving people. Jesus went to the well at a socially unacceptable time to find worship for his Father. He sought out the tax collectors, the prostitutes, and the adulteresses—sinners whom the world had already judged and cast aside. Those who worship Jesus in spirit and truth are saved and set free in spirit and in truth from every vain and destructive affair with this world. He allured the unlovable to himself. He remarried his long lost wife, and made her beautiful, clean, and desirable.

A FULL AND FOREVER HAPPINESS

Our love affairs with sin are not just a matter of morality, though, but of joy. This is not just about faithfulness to God, but about finding our deepest, most satisfying fulfillment. Many people think following Jesus means surrendering our happiness. You can either enjoy a fun, passionate, and exciting life here for a short time or live a bland, boring, but safe life forever with God. That lie is a quiet, but violent concentration camp, fencing men and women in, keeping them away from God, and torturing them with lesser pleasures that only lead to a swift and yet never-ending death. If you want to be truly happy—even in this life, surrounded by everything beautiful, fun, and exciting in this world—you want to be found with Jesus.

Experiencing the full life with Jesus, we say with David, "You have put more joy in my heart than they have when their grain and wine abound" (Ps. 4:7). We can be infinitely and enduringly more happy with Jesus than with anything or even everything in a world without him—even when that world is filled and overflowing with promotions and bonuses at work, on-demand television, all-you-can-eat sushi, grossly accessible pornography, always new and better technology, and countless other goods become gods.

The argument of this book is not just that God is a more morally or socially acceptable treasure, but that he will satisfy you more than anyone or anything else. Christianity is not merely or even mainly about correcting your bad habits, but about satisfying and fulfilling you in the deepest way possible, and therefore making God look as great as he is. Our hearts were designed to enjoy a full and forever happiness, not the pitiful temporary pleasures for which we're too prone to settle. Pride, envy, anger, sloth, greed, gluttony, and lust are all woefully inadequate substitutes for the wonder, beauty, and affection of God. As first hopes or dreams or loves, they are killjoys by comparison to Christ. They will rob you, not ravish you. They will numb you, not heal you. They will slaughter you, not save you.

Looking to little, temporary gods—these seven mistresses—for true and lasting happiness is a frantic and expensive treasure hunt for fool's gold. You lose far more than you will ever find. It's like scouring the pantry for a warm sweater, or searching the medicine closet for something to eat, or opening the refrigerator to find your favorite book. The map inscribed on our sinful soul will not lead any of us to truth, glory, or happiness. It will lead us in circles of "almost" and "good enough" until it sits by our hospice bed, holding our confused, disappointed, and hopeless hand as we drift off into hell. We have to wake up, scrap the old map, and grab the compass pointing true north, trusting that the God who formed our hearts knows how to fill them. We have to fight to find joy in the right places.

WE ARE AT WAR

The gospel is a story of a relentless romance *and* of fierce warfare. The promises written into Hosea's faithfulness, mercy, and love toward Gomer *are* fulfilled in Jesus. Peter writes:

But you are a chosen race, a royal priesthood, a holy nation, a people for his own possession, that you may proclaim the excellencies of him who called you out of darkness into his marvelous light. Once you were not a people, but now you are God's people; once you had not received mercy, but now you have received mercy. (1 Pet. 2:9–10, emphasis added)

The God who made heaven and earth has been treated by all mankind—every man and woman—as worse than a slave. Yet he abandons his throne to find his defiled bride, cleanse of her filth, and marry her to himself for all eternity. Anyone reading this story might think God is a reckless lover—a love-sick fool blinded by his devotion to a woman he cannot and should not trust. Husbands like him are trapped in a violent, broken cycle of heartbreak, regularly and hopelessly deceived, betrayed, and deserted. Not this Husband. No, what looks like blind devotion is an all-seeing, unstoppable commitment to his name and his bride—a family of undeserving, but chosen children. There's nothing reckless about a God who writes the story—beginning to end, every page—and then carries it out in unexplainable, relentless, and sovereign love.

Marriage is not the only metaphor Peter uses, though. In the very next verse, he writes, "Beloved, I urge you as sojourners and exiles to abstain from the passions of the flesh, which wage war against your soul" (1 Pet. 2:11). The bride who's been redeemed from her sin is still in a brutal battle against it. We are at war. Better, we are a living, breathing battlefield. The fierce warfare is happening within us (James 4:1). The desires we indulged before are hiding, plotting, and attacking the new desires we have for God and his holiness.

We are at war, but for believers, it is a war that's already been won. The enemies have been named and defeated, but they are still dangerous. The outcome is decided, but the war wages on, and the fighting is as fierce as ever. Jesus's victory at the cross wasn't meant to make us relax and put down our weapons. No, he died and rose to arm us with the invincible hope and power of his Spirit and promises. He went to Calvary so that we could kill our sin (Rom. 8:13).

Killjoys was written to lead you further into marriage with our God and further into war against your sin. The truths, warnings, and promises in these pages are meant to chart a path to greater holiness and greater joy. May God, "who is able to keep you from stumbling and to present you blameless before the presence of his glory with great joy" (Jude 1:24), receive all the recognition and glory as he brings to completion what he has started in you (Phil. 1:6).

A Brief History
of Iniquity

How the Deadly Sins Became Seven

RYAN GRIFFITH

"The use of fashions in thought is to distract men from their real dangers. We direct the fashionable outcry of each generation against those vices of which it is in the least danger, and fix its approval on the virtue that is nearest the vice which we are trying to make endemic. The game is to have them all running around with fire extinguishers whenever there's a flood; and all crowding to that side of the boat which is already nearly gone under." —C. S. Lewis, *The Screwtape Letters*

It is a strange distortion of history that the so-called seven deadly sins could be found fashionable in contemporary culture. But, knowing the corruption of the human heart, perhaps we should not be surprised by the 21st century's fascination with what's taboo. Witness (or better yet, don't!) the range of television programming, feature films, novels, and even restaurant chains branded with the seven deadly sins. This prurient curiosity with wickedness has made the church's warnings against it socially unpopular, even unacceptable. But sin only entertains as long as it is cheered by triviality and flaunted by deliberate ignorance. When sin is identified with devilish rebellion and the myriad disorders that disfigure human experience, such applause is repugnant. Sin, when appropriately named, loses its allure. And, like the taxonomy you learned in fifth-grade science, we need a tool to distinguish between *dog* and *golden retriever*—between *sin* and *censoriousness* (look that one up). Identifying a species of sin helps us address sin at its root. Historically, the classification of the *seven deadly sins* was designed centuries ago to do just that.

SEEING SIN AT ITS SOURCE

The seven *deadly* sins—pride, envy, anger, greed, sloth, gluttony, lust—are not so called because they are the most lethal. All sin is deadly. The reason the church has so long liked to talk about these *seven* sins (rather than 77 or 777) is because they represent the rest. More precisely, these seven sins have been considered the *sources of species* of sin—root-level sins from which a host of other sins often spring.

Down through the ages of the church, pastors and priests, monks and magistrates, bishops and bible study leaders have all wrestled with how to diagnose the sin-sick human heart. What, below the surface-level manifestation of a sinful behavior, is the real root idolatry? For example, what is at the core of a man's sinful impulse to secretly relish the misfortune of his neighbor? Or what is under a woman's relentless desire for more and more shoes?

This, at least, is what Evagrius of Pontus (346–399AD) wanted to know. Having been shaped by some of the greatest Christian minds of the 4th century, Evagrius spent the final 17 years of his life in a monastic community. As he taught and pastored, he observed that certain thoughts consistently plagued these devoted men. He eventually identified eight "thoughts" from which all other sins could be seen to flow—gluttony, impurity (lust), avarice (greed), sadness, anger, *acedia* (sloth), vainglory, and pride.[1] Identifying these patterns helped the community excise sin at its root, rather than superficially dealing with its manifestations.

DIAGNOSING THE DISEASE

Evagrius's disciple, John Cassian (360–430AD), brought this categorization into Western Christianity and noted that the eight could be placed on a continuum from carnal sin (gluttony) to spiritual sin (pride).[2] The diagnostic became part of the Latin monastic tradition and helped monks both identify patterns of sin and focus on cultivating corresponding virtues. Benedict of Nursia (c. 480–587AD), for example, developed a rule for monastic life that gave specific instructions for how to develop humility as an antidote to pride.[3]

The eight categories, however, became the familiar *seven* sins under the revision of Pope Gregory I ("the Great" 540–604AD). Based on a familiar book of Christian teaching, Gregory observed an organic relationship between pride as root and the sins of vainglory, envy, melancholy, sloth, avarice, lust, and gluttony as branches. In later church history pride and avarice would often vie for the distinction of being the

1   Evagrius, *The Praktikos and Chapters on Prayer*, trans. John Eudes Bamberger (Kalamazoo, MI: Cistercian Publications, 1972), 16.
2   John Cassian, *Conference of Abbot Serapion on the Eight Principal Faults* (*NPNF2* 11:339). For Cassian's development of the eight principal faults, see *The Twelve Books on the Institutes of the Cœnobia and The Remedies for the Eight Principal Faults* (*NPNF*[2] 11:233–290).
3   Benedict of Nursia, *The Rule of Saint Benedict in English*, trans. Timothy Fry (Collegeville: Liturgical Press, 1981), 32. See especially chapters 4 and 7.

"root" of all sin.[4] The manifestations of the seven sins, often called vices, then, could be seen as their fruit. The branch
of envy, for example, bore the fruit of "hatred, whispering,
detraction, exultation at the misfortune of a neighbor, and
affliction at his prosperity."[5] This structure served helpfully
with little amendment for several hundred years. As a rubric
for self-examination and an aid for confession, earnest Christians could trace the species of sin to their source and excise it
through repentance and the application of the gospel.

In the 13th century, scholastic theologian Thomas Aquinas (1225–1274) developed a distinction between *venial* and
mortal sins that would have significant impact on the Western church.[6] This, in part, developed from the understanding
that the seven could be placed on a spectrum from spiritual (e.g. pride) to carnal (e.g. lust). *Mortal* sins threatened to
sever *spiritual* life because, as Aquinas saw it, they were sins
against love. Mortal sin cut one off from the grace of the Holy
Spirit and, thus, separated a person from God and resulted
in eternal punishment. *Venial* sin offended and wounded love
and disposed a person to committing mortal sin, but only
resulted in temporal punishment.[7] Mortal sins like adultery

4   As he saw it, Gregory's reasoning was Scriptural, taking his cues from
the apocryphal text, Ecclesiasticus 10:14–15 (*Douay-Rheims*): "The beginning of the pride of man, is to fall off from God. Because his heart is de-
parted from him that made him: for pride is the beginning of all sin: he
that holdeth it, shall be filled with maledictions, and it shall ruin him in the
end." Gregory the Great, *Morals on the Book of Job*, The Latin Fathers of the
Christian Church, vol. 31 (Oxford: J. H. Parker, 1850) 33.45.87. Paul's teaching, however, should be regarded with greater authority—that "the love of
money is a root of all evils" (1 Tim. 6:10).

5   Gregory the Great, *Morals on the Book of Job*, 33.45.87–88.

6   See Aquinas, *Summa Theologica*, I–II.88.

7   See Aquinas, *Summa Theologica* I–II.72–89. The language above is
from the Catechism of the Roman Catholic Church, IV 1854–1864. Avail-

or theft were deliberate acts, demonstrating premeditation and consent of the will. Mortal sins sever one's relationship with God and result in eternal punishment. Venial sins like immoderate laughter or unwholesome speech, were neither grave nor premeditated and, as such, were forgivable—either through penance in life or purgation after death. The upshot of this distinction was that it highlighted *degrees* of sin—exaggerating about an accomplishment is not the same thing as taking someone's life.

The distinction, however, posed at least two dangers. First, it inferred that some sins (venial) are less condemnable than others (mortal). Thus, because of their willful and grave nature, the seven "capital" (from Latin, *caput*) sins earned the adjective 'deadly.' This ranking of sin obscured the fact that all sin, small or great, is rebellion. At its essence, sin is the declaration that something other than God is more to be desired than God. Thus, all sin is deadly because it is worthy of infinite judgment. Secondly, the mortal/venial distinction severed the relationship between root and fruit, disconnecting patterns of sinful behavior from the core idolatries of the heart. Thus, Aquinas's distinction weakened the diagnostic usefulness of the seven-sin taxonomy. Nevertheless, his distinction between venial and mortal sin has remained the doctrine of the Roman church to the present time.[8]

In the 16th century the Protestant reformers rejected Aquinas's distinction without completely abandoning the utility of the classification of seven root sins. The Reformation emphasis on *sola scriptura* and the fact that the seven

---

able online at http://www.vatican.va/archive/ccc_css/archive/catechism/p3s1c1a8.htm.

8   See the Catechism of the Roman Catholic Church, IV 1854–1864. See part two of Dante's *Divine Comedy* (*Purgatorio*) for an example of how Aquinas's philosophy and the seven deadly sins were understood in the following century.

capital sins were nowhere listed as such in the Bible, however, meant that the rubric was slowly abandoned in favor of other ethical approaches to diagnosing sin (applying, for example, Colossians 3:1–17). Surprisingly, contemporary Protestants probably make more mention of the seven deadly sins than many of their forebears.[9] This kind of categorization still threatens to encourage the idea that some sins are more or less serious, and may cause some to hold lightly or even dismiss certain other sins. As a diagnostic, though, the system holds great value, creating questions and categories that help us see and defeat our darkest inclinations.

SEVEN SINS, ONE HOPE

Diagnosing the root of sinful behavior entails identifying what we foolishly believe will make us more happy than joy in Christ. To make such a diagnosis, we need help—otherwise we will be running around with fire extinguishers when the boat is about to go under. Identifying seven especially deep, especially pervasive strains of sins will likely be helpful. Our only hope with any sin, however, is turn to God in Christ. "Search me, O God, and know my heart! Try me and know my thoughts! And see if there be any grievous way in me, and lead me in the way everlasting!" (Ps. 139.23–24). We must plead for the Spirit to do surgery on our hearts, revealing sin by the word (Eph. 6:17; Heb. 4:12). We must lean on close Christian friends who know us well and can help us repent, confess, and believe in the goodness and lovingkindness of Christ our Savior (James 5:16; Titus 3:3–7). Most of all,

---

9 For example, see these two excellent recently published books on the seven sins: Brian G. Hedges, *Hit List: Taking Aim at the Seven Deadly Sins* (Minneapolis: Cruciform Press, 2014) and Rebecca Konyndyk DeYoung, *Glittering Vices: A New Look at the Seven Deadly Sins and Their Remedies*, (Grand Rapids: Brazos, 2009).

we must remember that those who trust in Christ Jesus are no longer under sin's domain, but under the reign of Christ (Rom. 5:12–21; 8:1–4).

What we mustn't do is do nothing. All sin is deadly. As John Owen says, "Be always at it whilst you live; cease not a day from this work; be killing sin or it will be killing you."[10]

10   John Owen, *The Mortification of Sin in Believers*, vol. 6, The Works of John Owen (London: Banner of Truth Trust, 1965), 10.

Pride

JASON MEYER

Pride is a cosmic crime. It has the dubious distinction of standing alone atop the list of deadly sins. It is also "the essence of all sin."[11] As finite creatures, we cannot fully grasp God's infinite revulsion against pride's rebellion. God hates pride. What makes pride so singularly repulsive to God is the way that pride "contends for supremacy" with God himself.[12] Pride sets itself in opposition to God. The only fitting response is for God to oppose the proud (James 4:6; 1 Pet. 5:5). That is probably why pride is not simply another sin among many, but a sin in a category of its own. Other sins lead the sinner further away *from God*, but pride is particularly heinous in that it attempts to elevate the sinner *above God*.

The heinousness of pride means that it really does deserve to die. Pride, however, can be hard to spot, much less kill. Jonathan Edwards said pride is "the most hidden, secret, and deceitful of all sins."[13] What we need is a field guide for pride. This particular blueprint for victory surveys pride's var-

11   John Stott, quoted in C. J. Mahaney, *Humility: True Greatness* (Sisters, OR: Multnomah, 2005), 30.

12   C. J. Mahaney, *Humility*, 31. Mahaney notes that this expression came from Charles Bridges, but he does not quote the source.

13   Jonathan Edwards, *Advice to Young Converts*, quoted in C. J. Mahaney, *Humility*, 34.

ious forms and provides a clear line of sight so that we can place pride in our crosshairs and shoot to kill.

A FIELD GUIDE FOR PRIDE

Fighting pride is like fighting a shape-shifter. It can appear in forms that look like polar opposites: building up and tearing down. Here are six interrelated forms:

> *Building Up:* Self-Exaltation, Self-Promotion, and Self-Justification

> *Tearing Down:* Self-Degradation, Self-Demotion, and Self-Condemnation

The first three responses usually show up when we succeed and others fail. The latter three are more common when others succeed and we fail.

First, pride puts on the smug face of self-exaltation when success comes its way. Self-exaltation *takes credit* for the good things in our lives. Second, self-promotion is an extension of self-exaltation because it puts those good things forward so that others will *give us credit* for them. Third, self-justification is more specific in that it focuses on taking credit for morally good works as a way of being right before God or in the sight of others. Taking credit for being in the right makes it more likely that we will blame others for being in the wrong. The Pharisees displayed all of these species of pride. For instance, they paraded their self-righteousness before people to get praise from others (Matt. 6:1–2). Jesus said everyone who exalts himself (like a Pharisee) will be humbled (Matt. 23:12).

These three forms of pride all propose a toast to self, celebrating and showing off our successes. And they often raise their glasses with an acute awareness of the failures of others.

The Pharisees not only "trusted in themselves that they were righteous," but they also "treated others with contempt" (Luke 18:9).

Self-degradation, self-demotion, and self-condemnation all come when the shoe is on the other less fortunate foot. They emerge as we stew over our losses and others' successes. Rather than raising a toast to successes, these three forms of pride throw a lavish pity party. First, where self-exaltation elevates and builds up the self, self-degradation is a form of demolition which tears down the self. Second, self-demotion throws a public and pathetic party to highlight the fact that we have performed worse than others, we have it worse than others, or we have less than others. Self-demotion plans the funeral for our ego. Why would we want others to see these things? Ironically, self-demotion can be a sneaky form of self-promotion because we're actually fishing for the affirmation and reassurance we believe we deserve. Third, self-condemnation passes judgment on us when we fall short of our own standards. Sometimes we carry out the painful judgment on ourselves. We can mentally replay poor performances in order to beat ourselves up over our failures. Self-condemnation does not feel vindicated in the sight of others, but feels shame for falling short.

The common denominator for all six species of pride is self-preoccupation. Pride wants to be the center of attention: for good or for bad. Pride's fixation with self can only be countered with humility's forgetfulness of self. Humility is the photo-negative of pride.

PRIDE'S PHOTO NEGATIVE

We will begin killing pride when we experience more and more of pride's photo-negative: humility. If pride puts us in a position of opposition to God, then humility delights in taking a posture of dependence upon God. This posture of dependence puts us in a position to receive grace from God.

The apostle Peter expounds upon these points in illuminating ways. He says, "God opposes the proud, but gives grace to the humble" (1 Pet. 5:5). Next, he defines humility more spatially. Humility pitches its tent in a certain place: "under the mighty hand of God" (1 Pet. 5:6). Peter then answers the most obvious question: how can someone be humble? Answer: we humble ourselves by "casting all [our] anxieties on him" (1 Pet. 5:7). If pride stubbornly insists on carrying our own cares, then humility is quick to cast our cares on God. Humility even knows what to do when we don't know what to do: keep looking to him! When faced with impossible odds, king Jehoshaphat knows enough to look at the King Eternal and say, "we do not know what to do, but our eyes are on you" (2 Chron. 20:12).

In the quest for humility, we must be sure to avoid pride's counterfeit version of humility: self-deprecation. What's the discernable difference? Humility is not obsessed with tearing ourselves down. C. S. Lewis stated the distinction memorably: "Humility is not thinking less of ourselves, but thinking of ourselves less." In other words, humility is fundamentally a form of self-forgetfulness as opposed to pride's self-fixation. And humility's self-forgetfulness has a certain flavor: joy. It's not dour or sour. The joy of self-forgetfulness comes when a superior satisfaction in God overpowers our self-preoccupation. Humility does not join pride in treating others with contempt. We are too busy looking up at God's glory to look down on others or feel smug about ourselves. And unlike pride, humility does not have to be the center of attention. Humility is not self-promoting; it enjoys pointing out evidences of grace in others. It can celebrate their accomplishments.

But all of this talk about humility begs an important question: how can proud people ever be humbled? God gives us victory over pride through our Lord Jesus Christ. If pride is the essence of sin, then it is time to look at how we can have victory over sin. God lands three direct hits that kill pride decisively (conversion), then progressively (sanctification), and finally completely (glorification). All three hits require us to see rightly.

THREE BLOWS TO PRIDE'S EGO

1) Conversion: The Decisive Blow

The glory of God and the pride of man will collide at one of two crash sites: hell or the cross. In other words, either we will pay for our sins in hell or Christ will pay for our sins on the cross. Hell is the scene of a crash that never ends—a horror movie without credits. And every sinner deserves it. Justice says the story could end right there on that eternal note of terror.

But God, in his mercy, made another way. God sent his Son to vindicate the worth of his great name—the name sinners have defamed with their pride. Sin sends a blasphemous message that God's glory does not matter. If God failed to judge sin, then he would essentially send the same message: my glory does not matter. The death of Christ says, "God's glory matters *this* much! I am *this* committed to my glory." The sacrifice of Christ fully absorbs and satisfies the wrath of God. This glorious aspect of the atonement is called propitiation (Rom. 3:24–25). The fire of God's wrath falls on Christ at Calvary. This is the opposite of self-justification. The work of Christ is the sole ground of our justification. He justifies the ungodly (Rom. 4:5). Therefore, the cross is now the only safe place for the ungodly to stand before the final judgment.

The fire fell there once and will never fall there again. Sinners must cling to the cross to flee from the wrath to come.

The problem is that we are blind to his glory. The god of this age has put a blindfold over our eyes so that we cannot see the glory of Christ on the cross (2 Cor. 4:3–4). Conversion is a new creation work of God that overcomes our spiritual blindness and darkness. When Christ is proclaimed (2 Cor. 4:5), God floods our hearts with light so that the eyes of the heart are opened to see and savor the glory of God in the face of Jesus Christ (2 Cor. 4:6). The Spirit acts like a floodlight to illuminate the work of Christ on the cross.

This is the decisive moment when pride is crushed. Seeing the cross with these new eyes decisively defeats pride. Why? Those who see the cross rightly see themselves rightly. We see him on the cross, and we see our sin. The cross reveals what we deserve from God. We cannot receive the *grace of Christ* apart from seeing and embracing the undeserved *disgrace of Christ*. The cross decimates our proud pretensions and our smug, self-righteous sense of rightness before (and even above) God. The cross crushes us because it reveals the true nature of sin—its wickedness and gravity. It testifies to the greatness of our evil. If we were a little wicked, then there could be a small sacrifice. The immensity of the sacrifice, however, tells the immensity of our sin.

The song "Stricken, Smitten, and Afflicted" makes this point more poetically:

> *Ye who think of sin but lightly,*
> *Nor suppose the evil great,*
> *Here may view its nature rightly,*
> *Here its guilt may estimate.*
> *Mark the Sacrifice appointed!*
> *See Who bears the awful load!*

'Tis the Word, the Lord's Anointed,
Son of Man, and Son of God.

2) Sanctification: The Progressive Blow

This decisive work of crushing pride continues in sanctification with progressive blows against pride. Conversion sets us free to see the glory of Christ, which also sanctifies. There is no sightless sanctification. We're transformed from one degree of glory to the next *by beholding the glory of the Lord* (2 Cor. 3:18). So sanctification is also a struggle to see rightly. We need to see more clearly who God is and who we are.

Paul labored to help the pretentious Corinthians see. He makes this point in a shocking way in 2 Corinthians 12. Paul received stunning visions of heavenly glory, but surprisingly he was in danger of becoming conceited (2 Cor. 12:7). If this happened, he would fall into the trap of becoming like the false teachers who were marked by pride and arrogance (2 Cor. 11:18–21). Therefore, Paul received an incredibly painful thorn in the flesh in order to keep him humble (2 Cor. 12:7). Paul testified that he was not humbled *by the visions*—on the contrary he needed to be humbled *because of the visions* (2 Cor. 12:1-7). The shocking irony is that these were not visions of how great Paul was! Pride can even take great heavenly visions of God and twist them so that we think we are great for having received them. Pride is so twisted it can plagiarize and take credit for anything good—even vivid visions of God's glory.

This thorn was a torment to Paul. It was "in the flesh" (2 Cor. 12:7) which I take to mean that it wasn't outside the body. He experienced a deep and searing pain (i.e., torment). It was an affliction. Paul pleaded with the Lord three times to take it away (2 Cor. 12:8). But the Lord showed him that it served a purpose, a *good* purpose. Think about that statement for a second. God gave Paul chronic pain. Why? Paul needed chronic pain because his real problem was chronic pride. He needed to be humbled. Therefore, Paul received another vision: not a vision of heavenly glory, but a revelation of all-sufficient grace (2 Cor. 12:9).

Paul's response was to boast in his weakness (2 Cor. 12:9). None of us naturally responds that way. Why would anyone draw attention to his weaknesses? Could there be a greater contrast between pride and humility? He draws the gaze of others to his own weakness because Paul's weakness is the best backdrop against which others will see the beauty of God's strength. People will not see God or Paul rightly if Paul takes credit for what only God can do. Paul had to learn to regard weakness as a gift. If we are going to keep humbly leaning on God through faith, we need to see how great our need is and how great his grace really is. Feeling strong can lead to a cesspool of self-sufficiency and independence that leads us away from God. Feeling weak is the best garden for the flowering of dependence upon God's sufficient grace.

We need to see who we really are. One thing obscuring our vision is that we get mixed messages about maturity. It's true in this life here on earth that growing up means taking on more and more responsibility so that we become less and less dependent upon our parents. Spiritual growth, though, is actually the reverse. We don't become better and better so that we need God less and less. No, as we mature, we learn to grow more and more dependent upon our Heavenly Father. I learned this lesson in the adoption process. I had literally done everything I could. I had made all the phone calls and filled out all the paperwork and written all the emails. I am ashamed to say that it was not until that point that I started praying more. I had never felt so helpless and so out of control. God showed me that *the way I was feeling then was the way I was all the time.* My desperate need was always true, but not always felt. Control is such an illusion. It is good for us to feel viscerally how dependent we are spiritually, because then we will see the world and ourselves rightly. And a day is coming when we *will* see and feel rightly for all eternity.

3) Glorification: The Final Blow

Seeing the glory of God in its fullest—with all of our senses—will be the final blow to pride. The apostle John points us all to that blessed day: "Beloved, we are God's children now, and what we will be has not yet appeared; but we know that when he appears we shall be like him, because we shall see him as he is" (1 John 3:2).

My favorite verse of "Come Thou Fount of Every Blessing" helps put the glory of that day into the language of longing:

> *On that day when free from sinning, I shall see Thy lovely face!*
> *Full arrayed in blood-washed linen, how I'll sing Thy sovereign grace!*
> *Come, my Lord! No longer tarry! Bring Thy promises to pass!*
> *For I know Thy power will lead me till I'm home with Thee at last.*

How different it will be for those who did not have their pride killed decisively, progressively, and completely. God opposes pride actively and hates it passionately, which means that pride is spiritual suicide. Pride is on a collision course with God himself and the date is set. "For the Lord of hosts has a day against all that is proud and lofty, against all that is lifted up—and it shall be brought low" (Isa. 2:12). All must be torn down so that one thing alone may be left standing. "The

Lord alone will be exalted in that day" (Isa. 2:11). On that final day, the face of Christ will be a terror (Rev. 6:16–17) or a
treasure (1 John 3:2). This vision and conviction should send
us back into the present day to fight pride with even greater
humility and passion.

FIGHT SIN WITH SIGHT

"And everyone who thus hopes in him purifies himself as he
is pure" (1 John 3:3). The doctrine of heaven exists not just to
help us die well in the future, but to help us fight well today.
It is no wonder that 1 John 3:3 immediately follows 1 John 3:2.
I will let Martyn Lloyd-Jones explain:

> *There is a sense in which we can say that the whole object
> of verse 2 is to lead to verse 3, and if we fail to regard the
> second verse in that light, if we fail to see that its real ob-
> ject and purpose is to prepare the way for this third verse,
> then we have abused the second verse entirely, and we
> have failed to appreciate its true message to us. . . . You
> and I, having had a vision of glory, have to come down
> and translate it into practice and put it into daily opera-
> tion, and if it does not lead to that, then we are abusing
> the Scripture.[14]*

Ultimately, pride is a worship issue. We cannot think about
ourselves less unless we think about something else more.
The rivers of self-forgetfulness flow down from the Godward
heights of worship. He is the *only* God (1 Tim. 1:17) and the
only Sovereign (1 Tim. 6:15). No one can outlast God in foolish opposition because he is the King Eternal (1 Tim. 1:17).
God has opponents, but he has no rivals. He, and he alone, is
worthy of all worship and praise.

14   Martyn Lloyd-Jones, *Life in Christ* (Wheaton: Crossway, 1993), 296.

Therefore, God's children cannot be ambivalent about pride. We must hate it and hunt it down until its dead. The good news is that God's grace in us, his children, will kill pride decisively, progressively, and then completely. For our part, we must pray and ask the Spirit to open our eyes to more of God's glory, so that we are ever more in awe of him and ever less in awe of ourselves. The Bible's answer to our fallen self-obsession is a great work of grace in the gospel that creates in us a glorious obsession with God that climaxes in ever-increasing, everlasting worship. Thanks be to God that all pride will be consumed in that great flame of praise.

3

ENVY

JOE RIGNEY

Edmund Spenser, the 16th century poet, is most famous for composing *The Faerie Queene*, an allegorical poem about the Christian life. In the first book, Spenser's hero, the Red Cross Knight, encounters the seven deadly sins in the House of Pride. Envy is depicted as a man with cankered teeth, chewing on a venomous toad, poison running down his jaws.[15] He wears a many-colored robe, rides upon a ravenous wolf, and hides a deadly snake close to his chest.[16] Inwardly, he devours himself, weeping over the wealth of others and rejoicing in their misfortune. Envy grieves at the happiness of others and spews spiteful poison and abuse on those who practice faithful Christian obedience.

There's a long tradition of using vivid metaphors to describe various sins. For some reason, images of envy are especially grotesque. Envy is a green-ey'd monster, a ravenous

---

15 Edmund Spenser, *The Faerie Queene*, Book I, Canto IV. An excellent and accessible edition of the first book of Spenser's classic has been edited by Roy Maynard, *Fierce Wars and Faithful Loves: Book I of Edmund Spenser's The Faerie Queene* (Moscow: Canon Press, 1999).

16 Spenser depicts each sin performing actions that reflect the sin and riding on an appropriate beast: Sloth rides a lazy donkey, Gluttony a filthy pig, Lust a bearded goat, Greed a laden camel, Wrath a fierce lion, and Envy a ravenous wolf. Pride rides in a chariot that is pulled by the other six.

wolf, a beast with many heads. Envy is a gnawing worm, the rust of the heart, the malignant shriek of the shriveled soul. Envy chews on a venomous toad, drooling poison. Envy lies in wait and springs like a serpent when its prey is within range.

Envy cries over other's wealth. Envy cheers when another stumbles. Envy weeps at those who rejoice and rejoices over those who weep. Envy, as Solomon says, "makes the bones rot" (Prov. 14:30). It is no trifle, but a powerful force that can knock us off our feet. "Wrath is cruel; anger is overwhelming. But who can stand before envy?" (Prov. 27:4)

Who can stand before envy? The Christian Hedonist can, but only if we're alert to envy's seductive power and wage war on this enemy with all the power supplied by the gospel. We need to unmask envy's schemes and then bring the grace of God to bear so that we are freed from envy's venomous chains.

A PACK OF WOLVES

The first thing to do is to understand the nature of the foe— or foes, as the case may be. For envy, like all sins, hunts in a pack. It's always accompanied by a band of vicious wolves, and it's helpful to know and name this wolf-pack so that we can sniff out their stalking in our own lives. We begin with the alpha male himself. Envy is a feeling of unhappiness at the blessing and fortune of others. In the words of Merriam Webster, it is the painful and often resentful awareness of an advantage enjoyed by someone else.

We often lump envy and jealousy together, but there is an important distinction. Jealousy is oriented toward what we possess; envy is oriented toward the possessions of others. We are jealous for what we do not have (which is why jealousy is not always a sin); we are envious of what others have. Covetousness is an overweening desire for that which is not yours. Or, as I try to explain to my young boys, covetousness is wanting something so much it makes you fussy. Covetousness wants what the other guy has; envy is angry that the other guy has it. Covetousness is oriented toward your neighbor's possessions; envy toward the man himself.

Envy is similar to pride in that they're both rooted in the same self-will and selfish ambition. *Pride* is selfish rebellion when it occupies a superior position. *Envy* is the same impulse when it stands beneath another. Pride looks down on those below with smug and satisfied arrogance. Envy looks at those above with chafing hatred. *Rivalry* is competitiveness rooted in a proud and envious assessment of your own abilities and the abilities of others. *Resentment* is a simmering bitterness at some perceived injustice. The injustice may be as simple and twisted as a friend receiving an opportunity that you didn't. *Malice* is the suppressed hatred that plots and takes pleasure in the downfall of others. When you envy another, malice dreams and envisions their ruin and then gives a satisfied chuckle if the ruin comes to pass.

The common features in these sins are: (1) a distorted and corrupted desire, (2) a perverse comparison of oneself with others, (3) an ungodly preoccupation with the advantages of others, and (4) a smoldering anger at the blessings of others. Or to use the symptoms described in Brian Hedges' excellent treatment of envy, envy involves comparison, criticizing and complaining, ingratitude, and hatred.[17]

As helpful as definitions are, we need more than this if we're to put this wolf-pack down. For my own part, I've found that stories often unmask sin in ways that arguments

---

17   Brian Hedges, *Hit List: Taking Aim At the Seven Deadly Sins* (Minneapolis: Cruciform Press, 2014), 35–46. I cannot recommend Hedges highly enough. In addition to his accurate diagnosis and gospel-rooted treatment, Hedges includes many quotations and stories from history that vividly describe and depict envy.

from doctrine can't. King David would no doubt agree. Nathan's tale of the poor man and his sheep punctured the king's self-delusions and revealed his rebellion. When it comes to envy, the story of David and Saul in 1 Samuel 18–19 showcases envy's pack of wolves.

AN ENEMY WITH MANY FACES

David has just killed Goliath. When the army returns to Jerusalem, the women come out of the city "to meet King Saul" (1 Sam. 18:6). However, their song celebrates the accomplishments of both Saul *and* David. What's more, their song elevates the young warrior over the great king: "Saul has slain his thousands, but David his ten thousands" (18:7). The comparison provokes the king to envy. He thought this celebration was for him and can't stomach sharing the stage with the shepherd boy. As one commentator put it, Saul is the older brother at the prodigal's party. Even worse, he thought it was supposed to be his party, and so he gets angry at being upstaged.

Saul's envy begets rivalry. In verse 9, we're told that Saul "eyed David from that day on." He gave David the sidelong glance and begins to try to elbow him out. There is now a competition: who will be the greater warrior? Who will slay more enemies? Who will the people love and esteem more?

His rivalry is rooted in resentment as Saul grows bitter at the perceived injustice of the comparison: "They have ascribed to David ten thousands, and to me they have ascribed thousands." Resentment projects the comparison into the future and deepens the felt sense of injustice: "what more can he have but the kingdom?" (18:8). Saul's envy and rivalry pervert his imagination as he grieves at the present comparison and looks to the future with fear and outrage. Envy, rivalry, and resentment open the door to greater demonic influence as a harmful spirit rushes upon Saul and he begins to maliciously hope for David's downfall. More than that, he begins to plot and plan how to bring it about. Envy won't simply wait for ruin to come upon its rival; it must have an active hand in tearing him down.

The onset of Saul's malice helps us see how envy changes shape. When Saul first sees David's success, he takes him into his home (1 Sam. 18:2), and sets him over the men of war (18:5). Saul's first reaction to seeing God's hand on David is to give him a promotion. Then when envy is awakened, he grows erratic and tries to pin David to the wall with a spear. When David evades him, he grows fearful of him and sends him out of his house (18:13). When God continued to bless David, Saul stands in fearful awe of him (18:15). Then he begins to flatter David, offering him his daughter, while secretly plotting in his mind, "Let not my hand be against him, but let the hand of the Philistines be against him" (18:17).

When David shows his humility—"Who am I, and who are my relatives, my father's clan in Israel, that I should be son-in-law to the king?" (18:18)—Saul withdraws the offer, but continues his plotting. Later, when he discovers that his daughter Michal loves David, he thinks, "Let me give her to him, that she may be a snare for him and that the hand of the Philistines may be against him" (18:21). Perhaps he thinks in giving away his daughter that he will now have a spy in David's house. Maybe he thinks or even hopes that Michal will lead David astray in some way. Saul brings more people into the mix, using them to flatter David with lies about the king's delight.

When David again displays his humility—"Does it seem to you a little thing to become the king's son-in-law, since I am a poor man and have no reputation?" (18:23)— Saul's plots escalate and he offers to accept 100 Philistine foreskins instead of a bride-price. Why? "Now Saul thought to make David fall by the hand of the Philistines" (18:25). Saul hoped that killing 100 men single-handedly would prove too much for David. Instead, David brought back 200 and "Saul saw and knew that the Lord was with David and became even more afraid" (18:28–29). But this fear doesn't lead to reconciliation. Instead, Saul brings his hatred and malice into the open, telling his son and his servants that they should kill David (19:1).

HOW TO KILL YOUR DRAGON

Promotion, resentment, raving and erratic behavior, fear and awe, flattery and lies, false gifts and malicious plots, overt hostility and hatred. These are the many faces of envy and rivalry. As we try to evaluate our hearts, we need to be alert to the fact that envy is a chameleon, masquerading as smooth flattery one minute and righteous indignation the next, fear and awe one minute and then malicious plotting and public assault the next.

Saul's story also shows us that envy, like all sin, is fundamentally irrational. It's insane. When envy takes root in someone's heart, he or she does things that make no sense. Like seeing God's hand of blessing on someone in an obvious way, *knowing* that it is God's blessing, and still making that person an enemy (1 Sam. 18:28–29). Envy is myopic; it focuses the mind on the offense of the other person's success so that all other considerations take a backseat, and it spirals down into despair and destruction.

Therefore, as we address the sin of envy, we're talking about a whole host of sins: envy, jealousy, covetousness, rivalry, resentment, malice, hatred, flattery, corrupt desire, smoldering anger, perverse comparison, a fixation on the blessing of other people.

SEEING WITH THE EYES OF ENVY

How then does envy operate? What are its inner workings? First, *envy follows success*, like night follows day. What provokes envy in Saul is God's hand of blessing on David. He defeats Goliath, seemingly against all odds. He was successful wherever Saul sent him (1 Sam. 18:5). He was loved by many: by Saul's son (18:1-3), by the people, by Saul's servants, by Saul's daughter (18:20), by all Israel and Judah (18:16). God was with him (18:12) so that he had success "in all of his undertakings" (18:14) and in all of his battles with the Philistines. The narrator caps off David's triumphs by saying that he had "more success than all the servants of Saul so that his name was highly esteemed" (18:30).

Envy follows success with a hungry eye, incessantly asking questions like, "What about me?" or "Why not me?" It can stomach other people's success to a point, which is why envy co-opts them and invites them into his or her home. But as soon as the newcomer begins to overshadow the host, envy turns like a ravenous wolf and gnaws itself into malice and seeks the ruin of the more successful.

Second, *envy operates close to home*. It attacks our closest relationships first. It makes fellowship thorny, difficult, and sometimes even impossible. We tend to envy those who are close at hand, who are like us, and who care about the same things that we do. Most young pastors don't envy John Piper or Tim Keller or Al Mohler. While we certainly admire and respect them, we are not grieved by their fruitfulness and success because we put these men in a class of their own. Instead, we envy those whom we regard as our peers, or those a few steps ahead of us. As novelist Joseph Heller put it, "There is no disappointment so numbing . . . as someone no better than you achieving more."

Saul's envy is awakened when he brings David *into his own house* (1 Sam. 18:2). For us, envy rears its ugly head when a friend or peer makes better grades, has more friends, is more likeable, receives a promotion, is given more opportunities, or better opportunities. It emerges when they are better-looking or a better parent, when they are more educated, more gifted, more popular, more intelligent, more esteemed, or more successful.

Third, *envy involves mimetic desire* ("mimetic" comes from the Greek word for *imitation*). Envy is a corrupted form of desire and imitation. Simple desire involves a subject and an object, a person desiring and an object desired. Mimetic, or triangular, desire involves a subject, an object, and a model who gives the object its value. It involves a person desiring, an object desired, and, most importantly, another person who makes the object desirable *by desiring it first*.

Imagine a room full of toy animals and a small child in the middle happily playing with a black horse. A second child walks into the room. Which toy does the second child want? Right, the black horse. Why is that? Because the first child is already happily playing with it. It's the model's desire that makes the toy desirable.

Now, before the second child came in, the first child could have happily put the black horse down in order to play with the brown cow, but now he won't. Why? Because the second child's desire for the black horse has confirmed and reinforced that this is in fact the best toy. The second child has also become a model, leading to the tug-of-war experienced by every parent in the history of the world—one of the few experiences for which parents are not tempted to envy each other.

And this triangular desire is found not only in the hearts of toddlers. It explains why two roommates will wreck a long friendship competing for the attention of the same girl. It explains why two co-workers will destroy a long partnership over a big client. It explains advertising, branding, and the willingness of people to pretend to enjoy things that they hate because someone that they admire enjoys it. It explains why a king who craves the esteem of his people would try to pin a young hero to the wall because he heard some women sing a song.

Triangular desire is a corrupted form of imitation in which we move from wanting to *be like* our model, to *competing with* our model, to seeking *to replace* our model. It's not that we merely want what the model has; we want to be the model. When the second child sees the first child playing, he doesn't mainly want the toy. He wants the experience of joy that the first child is experiencing. If the first child gave up the black horse and began to play happily with the brown cow, the second child would now crave the brown cow. Which is why the envious are so unhappy. The harder they try to compete and the more deeply they lust for the happiness of another, the more it eludes them.

HUNTING THE WOLVES IN US

So, we have seen the many faces of envy. We've seen the way that envy operates in our hearts—following success, assaulting our closest relationships, and corrupting our desire to be like those we admire. If we're going to diagnose ourselves, though, we not only need to see envy's ugly face, but its glorious opposite as well. In the story of David and Saul, envy's opposite is Saul's son, Jonathan.

Jonathan had every reason to fear, envy, and compete with David. David's victory over Goliath is a threat to Jonathan's future throne. But Jonathan doesn't resent David's success. Jonathan recognizes the hand of God and the blessing of God and the presence of God on David, and Jonathan simply wants to be near him. Unlike Saul, David's nearness doesn't provoke rivalry and malice. The song of the women doesn't produce resentment and displeasure. Instead, it produces deep love and admiration.

Jonathan loves David. He *loves* David. He receives God's blessing of David as a blessing to himself. He loves David as he loves his own soul. He doesn't want to replace David, but to covenant with David, to be bound to him as a friend and comrade. He removes his royal robe and his armor and gives it to David as a gift, anticipating David's kingship. He advocates for David, shelters David, and supports David against his father. In fact, later in 1 Samuel 23:17, Jonathan says to David, "You shall be king over Israel and I shall be next to you."

The difference between Saul and Jonathan enables us to test ourselves for envy. This is the test: How do you respond to the blessing and success of others? Do you murmur and gossip about it, or do you celebrate with them? Are you filled with gratitude, or carping rivalry? When it comes to the success and fruitfulness of others, are you their biggest fan or their biggest critic?

> *Pastors*, if another church in your town is fruitful with the gospel, what will you do? Will you grumble about it? Will you be filled with envy because so many people—perhaps even some who used to attend your church—go to that church or listen to that pastor?

> *Unmarried folks*, when your friend gets a girlfriend or boyfriend, or gets engaged, or gets married, are you genuinely happy for them? Are you filled with gratitude that God has brought them such a wonderful blessing? Or inwardly are you carping about the fact that you've been passed by once again?

Young people, how do you respond when your friends and siblings are blessed by God? When they make the team or get an award or have lots of friends, are you happy for them? Do you communicate how excited and proud you are of them when they are blessed by God? Or do you eye them with resentment and displeasure?

Moms, what is your reaction when someone else's child succeeds? Are you thrilled when someone else's baby learns to walk before yours or learns to talk before yours? Are you constantly eyeing other moms like Saul eyed David, feeling anger and displeasure when God blesses their parenting? Do you murmur about other mothers behind their backs?

Men, how do you react when someone else gets a promotion at work? If you were the general in Saul's army replaced by the young shepherd kid from Bethlehem, what would your reaction be? Would you throw your whole weight behind him? Or would you be tempted to undermine his authority and leadership?

THREE ENEMIES OF ENVY

If we test ourselves and fail, what hope do we have? Much in every way. We have the cross of Christ. We have the grace of God. We have the deep joy and gladness of knowing God in Christ. Let's briefly unpack each of these.

1) The Cross of Christ

The only way to destroy envy is through the cross of Jesus Christ. The blood of Christ alone cleanses us from the sins of

envy, rivalry, resentment, and malice. Jesus died to set us free
from all of envy's chains. We must confess our sins, genuinely
seek to turn from them, asking God for help, and trusting in
Christ alone to forgive our sins and to meet all of our needs.

2) *The Grace of God*

Paul says, "By the grace of God I am what I am" (1 Cor. 15:10).
Grace is what defines us. Grace is what forms and fill us.
Grace is what makes us who and what we are. You don't need
all those things that others have; you have grace! You have
God. And he approves of you. He is happy with you because
of what Christ has done. He embraces you as his sons and
daughters. He says to you: *You are my beloved child, I am well-
pleased with you.* If you believe this deep in your heart, you
can be free from envy.

3) *Gratitude for Our Blessings and Others'*

Because we are defined by the grace of God, we can give
thanks always and for everything. Because we know that God
has given us his Son Jesus and will one day give us all things
(Rom. 8:32), even now we can be filled with gratitude for all
of his good gifts to us. As Brian Hedges writes, "The most
effective medicine for envy is the pure spiritual milk of God's
goodness."[18] Gratitude is the posture of the soul that receives
this goodness. And gratitude is fundamentally incompatible
with envy. Grateful people do not envy; indeed they cannot.
Those who's hearts are overflowing with thankfulness to God
for all of his kindness toward them have no room for envy's
pack of wolves, with all of its ugly faces.

But we ought not stop with God's kindness to us. We
should also be thankful for what God gives to others. This is

18   Hedges, *Hit List*, 44.

a true sign of the new heart: when you look at what God gives
to other people (and not to you) and say "Thank you, Thank
you, Thank you, Lord, because you have been so kind to them
and so kind to me." In the end, God's glad-hearted approval
of us in Christ is what frees us from being defined by the
blessings and opportunities of others. God's warm-hearted
embrace of us in his Son delivers us from petty enslavement
to envy, so that we can enjoy and celebrate the gifts and abilities of our friends and family. The soul-enlarging grace of
God enables us to say:

> *I do not need to grasp for the talents and gifts of oth-*
> *ers. I do not need to covet my neighbor's spouse, house,*
> *family, ministry, or opportunities. I am not defined by*
> *the blessings of others; I am defined by the grace of God.*
> *Therefore, I will refuse to measure myself by a false stan-*
> *dard. I will resist the compulsive and relentless urge to*
> *compete with everyone under the sun (especially those*
> *who are called to do the same things that I am). I will*
> *put to death malicious dreams about the downfall and*
> *failure of others by savoring the sure knowledge that God*
> *is lavish in grace and that he has promised to graciously,*
> *freely, and abundantly give to me and to them all things*
> *in his Beloved Son.*

4

Anger

JONATHAN PARNELL

"What do you have to be angry about?" Sometimes in the Bible, God's own words to an individual are pervasively relevant to all of us. God's question to Jonah—the perturbed prophet—is a word we need to hear.

As the story goes, God relented from the disaster aimed at Nineveh. That made Jonah unhappy. "It displeased Jonah exceedingly, and he was angry" (Jonah 4:1). At this point, the readers are let in on the real truth behind Jonah's actions, and really, the whole conflict of the narrative. The reason the reluctant prophet ended up in the belly of the whale, and the reason the storm came while he was at sea, and the whole reason he was bound for Tarshish instead of Nineveh to begin with, is because Jonah knew something about the character of God. "That is why I made haste to flee to Tarshish [rather than preach to Nineveh]; for I knew that you are a gracious God and merciful, slow to anger and abounding in steadfast love, and relenting from disaster" (Jonah 4:2).

This is a sad resolution to a roller-coaster tale—and it unravels with anger. Jonah didn't want to preach repentance to the godless city of Nineveh because he didn't want the Ninevites to repent. He didn't want them to know God's mercy, and *that they did* made him mad. *Anger*, therefore, becomes the tragic climax of this drama. It's the emotion that steps on stage and pulls the mask off God's demented messenger. *Anger* tells us what's really happening—both in Jonah's heart and our own.

TOWARD THE MEANING OF ANGER

Anger makes the list of the seven deadly sins because for centuries people have witnessed its destructive power and influence. Understanding anger gets much more complicated than simply looking at its effects, though. Anger isn't merely a sin that causes chaos, it's an *emotion* that is indicative of something deeper—something in the subconscious desires of the human heart. This begins the hard, but critical work of digging beneath the surface to find the *root-sin*[19] of anger.

There is nothing inherently Christian, or even spiritual, in understanding that anger is a whistle-blower for a deeper, darker devotion in the soul. Even recent secular literature about anger makes this very point. In her book, *The Gift of Anger* (modestly subtitled "Seven Steps to Uncover the Meaning of Anger and Gain Awareness, True Strength, and Peace"), Marcia Cannon explains, "You become angry when you define reality as unacceptable and you feel unable to easily correct it, tolerate it, or let it go."[20] Notice that the emphasis in this statement is on the context of anger—"reality" as it is experienced and defined by you. Anger is only symptomatic of *something else*—circumstances we consider unacceptable. Which means, anger is inherently reactionary, not original. As Cannon would suggest, we gain insight into anger by looking at *that unacceptable thing* to which anger responds.

---

19   Jack Miller, *Repentance: A Daring Call to Real Surrender* (Fort Washington: CLC Publications, 2010), 15.
20   Marcia Cannon, *The Gift of Anger: Seven Steps to Uncover the Meaning of Anger and Gain Awareness, True Strength, and Peace* (Oakland: New Harbinger Publications, 2011), 17.

NO RESPECTER OF AGE

But before we get to the cause of anger, let's look at three de-scriptors of anger that make it unique in comparison to other sins. Just like every other sin, anger "is a culpable and personal affront on a personal God,"[21] but it does have its own layers of distinctiveness and complexity.

First, anger, like pride, is among the most widespread sins. To be sure, "all have sinned" (Rom. 3:23), but we might say more particularly, "all have been angry." From a cultural-historical perspective, recall that the first evidence of sin's devastation in the world was an angry meltdown. Early in Genesis, Cain reacted badly when God rejected his sacrifice. "So Cain was very angry, and his face fell" (Gen. 4:5). And how does God confront him? He asks the central question of this chapter: "*Why* are you angry, and why has your face fallen? (Gen. 4:6). God wants us to find the root.

Anger is widespread because it's been here since the first things went wrong. The sins of our first ancestors have per-vaded every generation ever since. The breadth of anger is omni-cultural-historical (all peoples in all times), and om-ni-generational (all ages). Could anger be the first sin we each commit? Have you ever heard an infant cry? Surely this doesn't apply to the children in your life, but speaking for my own, in-fused in their earliest shrills is an all-consuming rage. If they had hands as big and functional as ours, there's little doubt they'd wrap them around our necks and squeeze. Children, even infants, can definitely "define reality as unacceptable"— and they insist that everyone around them knows it. Whether the kids are hungry or someone isn't sharing Rainbow Dash,[22]

21   Cornelius Plantinga, *Not the Way It Is Supposed to Be: A Breviary on Sin* (Grand Rapids: Eerdmans, 1995), 13.
22   Rainbow Dash is a fictional character (and toy figurine) from the car-toon series My Little Pony.

all parents have seen enough red-faces smeared with tears to know that anger meets us all while we're young. Moreover, we never outgrow it. There's no denying the moments when parents find their own faces red and voices raised, reminding us that adults can morph into four-year-olds when we don't get our way. Anger is no respecter of age.

Some personalities, it has been said, tend toward red-faced eruptions; others are unflappably relaxed and easy-going. But the truth is, as Neurophysiologist Nerina Ramlakham explains, everyone gets angry, it's just expressed in different ways. "Now we separate people differently into those who hold rage in and those who express it out."[23] There are rage-containers and rage-spewers, but in both cases, there is rage. All have been angry, some loudly and violently, others quietly and secretly.

MORE DEADLY THAN THE OTHERS

Second, anger is the most dangerous of the deadly sins. Again, to be clear, "the wages of [all] sin is death" (Rom. 6:23), but the uninhibited expression of anger can quite literally kill—physically, the object, and spiritually, the subject. Jesus connects our anger with murder. "You have heard that it was said to those of old, 'You shall not murder; and whoever murders will be liable to judgment.' But I say to you that everyone who is angry with his brother will be liable to judgment" (Matt. 5:21–22). Bavinck comments, "Jesus says that not just the deed, but even the first upsurge of illegitimate anger—even if not expressed in a single word—made people liable to judg-

---

23   Victoria Lambert, "Why Anger Is Bad for You" in *The Australian*, 14 March 2014, http://www.theaustralian.com.au/news/world/why-anger-is-bad-for-you/story-fnb64oi6-1226854026035

ment."²⁴ Murder and anger are joined on the same continuum, and so closely related that Jesus considers them virtually equivalent. In light of God's judgment, murder and anger are merely different forms of the same condemnable offense. As the apostle John would later write, "Everyone who hates his brother is a murderer" (1 John 3:15).

Beyond this deadly association and the fact that unrighteous anger is a violent degradation of a holy life, anger can cause calculated and uncalculated harm to others. All agree that angry, premeditated harm, should be punished. But anger can also be so spontaneous and uncontrollable that it leads people to commit crimes they never would have imagined themselves doing. The American justice system has a category for this: crimes of passion. It involves an assault that happens as the result of a sudden impulse—when the perpetrator is so inebriated by his or her emotions that he or she makes a foolish decision. If it is proven that an assault was instigated by rage—as opposed to being premeditated—our modern justice system considers it a lesser offense. The court actually has some empathy for the impulsively and violently angry. This testifies to the idea that anger can be both intoxicating and ubiquitous. Most understand the disorienting power of anger, and most know it enough to sympathize at some level with those who experience and even wield it.

THE GOOD, THE BAD, THE ANGRY

Third, not all anger is sin. Anger itself is a name for something that may be evil *or* good, wicked *or* righteous. After all, anger distinguishes itself from the other deadly sins in one significant way: *God gets angry.* God's anger is all over the pages of

24   Herman Bavinck, *Reformed Dogmatics: Sin and Salvation in Christ,* vol. 3 (Grand Rapids: Baker Academic, 2005), 154.

Scripture. As the psalmist says, "God is a righteous judge, and a God who feels indignation every day" (Ps. 7:11).

And more than simply feeling it, God *executes* his anger in judgment, which is why Moses prayed after the golden calf incident, "Turn from your burning anger and relent from *this disaster against* your people" (Ex. 32:12). Furthermore, far from Marcion's fatal error, this wrath fumes throughout the whole Bible, Old and New Testaments. According to Paul, it is actually Jesus himself who will return one day to finally and fully execute the divine anger, "inflicting vengeance on those who do not know God and on those who do not obey the gospel of our Lord Jesus" (2 Thess. 1:8). Even during Jesus's earthly ministry, when he was confronted by the obstinate Pharisees, "He looked around at them *with anger*, grieved at their hardness of heart" (Mark 3:5).

Therefore, if God gets angry (Rom. 1:18), and God never sins (James 1:13; Heb. 4:15), then anger—when expressed rightly—necessarily must not be sin. We must look then to the motivations for anger—the responses angry people have to the realities around them—to begin to understand the anger of sinful human beings and how it differs from God's righteous wrath. Cannon writes, "Your anger comes up automatically when you need help to deal with a perceived threat or in seemingly tough situations that you don't feel powerful enough to handle calmly and easily."[25] Clearly this definition is not describing God's reasons for being angry. God is all-powerful and never reacting out of a sense of helplessness. But, as Cannon indicates, human beings react from a far more vulnerable position. Both God and man experience anger, but it is the cause of anger, not the experience of it, that qualifies it as *sinful* or *righteous*. "What do you *have* to be angry about?"—that really is the question.

---

25   Cannon, *The Gift of Anger: Seven Steps to Uncover the Meaning of Anger and Gain Awareness, True Strength, and Peace* , 7.

WHAT'S LOVE GOT TO DO WITH IT?

What we *have* to be angry about can be reduced down to one issue: love. Sometimes, we gain more insight into a particular sin by understanding its holy counterpart—by comparing vices and virtues. For example, we can examine pride through the lens of humility or expose greed with the light of generosity. Anger, however, isn't as symmetrical. We might assume that the opposite of anger is love, but actually, the opposite of anger is indifference. "In its uncorrupted origin," explains Tim Keller, "anger is actually a form of love."[26] Anger is how we respond to whatever threatens someone or something we care about. How we perceive and respond to reality has to do with what we value. Anger is love in motion to protect the object of our love. If we want to know *what* we have to be angry about, we should look to the objects of our affection. And if we want to know when anger is sinful, we look for how our loves have become distorted.

This explains why the problem of anger is so pervasive. Humans are fundamentally lovers, as James K. A. Smith puts it: ". . . [T]he way we inhabit the world is not primarily as thinkers, or even believers, but as more affective, embodied creatures who make our way in the world more by feeling our way around it."[27] We are always hopelessly in love with something, even if we are not aware of it. The question isn't *whether* we love, but *what* we love. Smith continues, "What really defines us is what we love—what we long for; what we desire.[28]

26 Tim Keller, "The Healing of Anger," preached 17 October 2004 at Redeemer Presbyterian Church, New York, available online at http://www.gospelinlife.com/the-healing-of-anger-5464.html.

27 James K. A. Smith, *Desiring the Kingdom: Worship, Worldview, and Cultural Formation, Cultural Liturgies* (Grand Rapids: Baker, 2009), 47.

28 James K. A. Smith, *Discipleship in the Present Tense: Reflections on Faith and Culture* (Grand Rapids: Calvin College Press, 2013), 181.

Indeed, *we are what we love*. Seventeenth-century theologian Henry Scougal puts it this way: "The worth and excellency of a soul is to be measured by the object of its love."[29] Therefore, because we interpret reality fundamentally as lovers, and because threats to what we love exist at every turn, reasons to be angry emerge everywhere all the time.

Confronted with so much temptation, we see again and again, humans are not only lovers, but *broken lovers*. This brokenness is seen in our disordered loves, or as Augustine called them, our "inordinate affections." We were created to love God most and best, but too often we prefer ourselves and the things that serve us. Here is the age-old problem that curves us in on ourselves and hoists up good things as ultimate things. Here is where anger goes haywire—where it leaves all semblance of righteousness and becomes evil. We wish that the only thing that made us angry was the careless delivery guy who speeds down our street while our kids are playing in the front yard, or the horrific injustices of terrorism or slavery, because we know these things anger God, too. But too often, we find ourselves getting annoyed at the simplest, most unjustified things—things like a withering plant on a sunny day (Jonah 4:9).

Sinful anger, therefore, is inherently stupid. It happens when we *misperceive* reality as unacceptable, when we are so blinded by our self-consumed loves that we want to annihilate anything that doesn't serve us. Sinful anger happens when, instead of imitating God, we try to play God by assuming the right to draw the lines, defining what should or should not be. In sinful anger, we respond in a manner disproportionate to the facts, forcing everyone around us to interpret the world on our terms, based upon what *we* love most—which is too often the object in the mirror.

---

29   Quoted in John Piper, *The Pleasures of God: Meditations on God's Delight in Being God* (Colorado Springs: Multnomah, 2012), 2.

Unrighteous anger is, to adjust a few words of a well-known phrase, *the explosive power of a flawed affection.* Tim Keller gives an example,

> *There's nothing wrong with getting angry to a degree if somebody slights your reputation, but why are you ten times—a hundred times—more angry about it than some horrible injustice being done to people in another part of the world?*
>
> *Because . . . if what you're really looking to for your significance and security is people's approval or a good reputation or status or something like that, then when anything gets between you and the thing you have to have, you become implacably angry. You have to have it. You're over the top. You can't shrug it off.*[30]

Truth is, if we press in behind the normal instances of our anger, it's ugly. If we find ourselves unusually perturbed about getting snubbed in social media, or being cut off in traffic, or going unrecognized for work, or having an idea shot down, or feeling under-appreciated by our spouse, it is likely because we love ourselves too much. Sinful anger is the result of our disordered loves, often our shameless self-love. The end of our anger only comes by shalom in our souls—a recalibration of our greatest love and devotion.

A METHOD AGAINST THE MADNESS

Just like with every other sin, unrighteous anger does not reign over hearts transformed by God's grace (Rom. 6:14). There is a way of escape (1 Cor. 10:13), though the path may not always be easy to find or simple to navigate. Defeating anger requires us to untangle the source of our anger—our

30 Keller, "The Healing of Anger."

perceptions of reality. It can be a difficult, even infuriating task, but these three steps provide one method against the madness.

1) *Analyze anger early.*

We must get to the source of anger as quickly as possible. When we find ourselves growing angry—when stress starts to rise and tempers begin to flare—we must hear God's words: *What do you have to be angry about?* Stop and ask: What is so important to me that I get this defensive and emotional? What am I loving so much that my heart is moved to feel this angry?

Interrogating our affections is the best way to mute misplaced aggression. One practical way this plays out in my life is in parenting. The most consistent cause of my anger is the disobedience of my children. On one hand, it is right to be appropriately incensed by their foolish behavior. I love them, and the trajectory of their foolishness is harm. But on the other hand, *their* disobedience isn't always the real issue. The tricky question is whether I am angry because I've been inconvenienced by their disobedience. If I am loving my children more than myself, my anger responds to their disobedience with patient and particular care and discipline. They are the objects of my love and my anger is meant to deal with the threat that foolishness makes against their flourishing. But if I'm mainly concerned with myself, my anger is not love for them; it only deals with the inconvenience their disobedience is *to me.* It is impulsive, near-sighted, curved in on what is best for me, not my children. I am loving myself at that moment, not my children.

Anytime anger steps into the room, the first question must be: *What do you have to be angry about? Who* am I loving right now? *Who* do I truly care about?

2) Feel ridiculous for your ridiculousness.

We should feel sorrow for our sin. If we ask the question about the love beneath our anger, Tim Keller says, "more often than not you'll immediately be embarrassed because many times the thing you're defending is your ego, your pride, your self-esteem." Oftentimes, our anger says we are self-centered and ridiculous, and we desperately need to hear that. At best, we'll be embarrassed. At worst, we will despair. It is painful to open the lid of our own hearts to find this kind of corruption.

As twisted as our hearts might be, though, we can face the darkness with a bold and hope-filled sorrow. We are bold because the corruption, real and present as it might be, cannot condemn us or defeat us. If we are in Christ, he has paid the price for our disordered loves. He bore the wrath we deserved, freeing us from sin's guilt. He rose from the dead, empowering us over sin's dominion. We are rightfully sad for how slow our souls are in receiving God's grace. We are sad that we find ourselves more perturbed by our wounded ego than we are by the abortions that take place downtown, that we shake our fists at rude media more than we lift our hands to heal the broken, that we inwardly mock those who disagree with us more than we publicly defend the rights of the voiceless. We are deeply sad about these things with a kind of serious sadness that isn't content to leave things there. We are grieved into repentance (2 Cor. 7:9–10). When we really get to the bottom of our self study, we are sad that we are angry in ways we should not be, and at the same time are not angry at what angers God. It is then that we turn and say, *No more, Lord. Please, no more.* And we know that he is able to arouse right anger and bring wrong anger to death in our heart.

3) Remember and imitate the anger of God.

Anger is love in motion to protect the object of our love. The driver's seat of anger is the affections, and if we're ever to understand why we become angry, we must look inside our hearts. This requires faith-filled probing and careful analysis. The motives behind anger are often mixed and rarely obvious. But it's never this way with God. God's anger always flows from pure and holy motives, and it always demonstrates his perfect love.

God *is* love, and above all things, he loves the shining forth of his character. He loves when the truth of his heart is on display—when *who he is* is *what we see*. The good news for us is that *seeing him* is precisely what makes us most happy. It's why we were made. Our souls are meant to behold his glory, to bask in his worth, to be satisfied in his perfections. God loves most to show us *this*. Our souls crave *this* most—to see, digest, and display *his glory*.

In other words, God's relentless commitment to his glory means that God is most committed to the very thing that brings us most joy. Therefore, every expression of his anger is a precise move to defend his glory *and* our joy. Neither arbitrary nor capricious, God's wrath is a calculated, effective response to eliminate the enemies of our everlasting good. The supreme example of this anger is seen in the cross of Jesus, planned before the world began (Rev. 13:8), executed against tremendous obstacles (Matt. 4:1–11), and dramatically, irrevocably successful (Isa. 53:11).

Our best means to fight sinful anger is to remember the anger of God—to remember his love and to what cost he has gone to end all threats against it. It's only there, when we see God's love—when we align our loves with his—that our anger can be sanctified. Loving like he loves is the only chance our anger has of being right. "What are you really angry about?" We should answer with the things that attack the glory of God. Over time, and finally on the last day, that kind of love will produce right anger, and end all wrong anger.

The antidote to anger isn't placid Stoicism or cool indifference; it's loving like crazy what is most loveable. The demise of sinful anger starts with our relentless pursuit to be enthralled by God—to be overcome with him, and then to be moved by him to value all that he values. We say "no" to sinful anger and it's pattern of consuming us as we say "yes" to God's wonder and allow ourselves to be more and more consumed by him.

5

Sloth

TONY REINKE

My kids love to draw the attention of zoo animals. From screeching at the monkeys to feeding the fish, they spend the most time with the animals that respond and interact. They walk right past the sloth. Slumped in the nook of a tree branch, the sloth just sits there, clueless to the world around him and careless about anything but controlling his comfort.

In the Christian life, sloth is not a prettier picture. With soul-decaying apathy and carelessness toward others, sloth rightly takes its place among the seven deadly sins. It looks like simple laziness, but sloth is a complex sin expressed in three persons: the sluggard, the workaholic, and the zombie.

THE SLUGGARD

The most familiar expression of sloth is idleness. The book of Proverbs names the slothful *sluggard*, and tries to wake him up with startling biblical images. "Go to the ant, O sluggard," the Proverb directs. The ant has no need to be prodded into activity, nor a reminder to diligently prepare and gather food. Then there's the blunt warning: "a little sleep, a little slumber, a little folding of the hands to rest, and poverty will come upon you like a robber, and want like an armed man" (Prov.

6:6–11).[31] Striking pictures of sloth, and warnings against it, are all over the Bible:

> *Through sloth the roof sinks in, and through indolence the house leaks (Eccles. 10:18).*

> *If anyone is not willing to work, let him not eat (2 Thess. 3:10).*

Slackhandedness is a cancer in the local church, and the sluggard should be warned and treated as an appropriate threat (2 Thess. 3:6–15). On the other hand, Jesus celebrates wise financial planning (Matt. 25:16–30). In short, God is concerned that we live diligently, not idly, with our finances, vocations, and time.

THE WORKAHOLIC

It's easy to see sloth in idleness, but there's another, more surprising example of sloth. A solid career is important, but vocational diligence can co-exist with apathy to asking, seeking, and knocking in the pursuit of eternal life (Matt. 7:7–14).

Workaholism is slothful because it uses labor in a self-centered way to focus on personal advancement or accumulated accolades. In God's economy, work is not a showcase for self, but a means for supporting others. Vocation is love intent on meeting others' needs. The workaholic who works himself ragged to prove himself superior to his neighbor, or to have

---

31 This is not to suggest poverty is the only result of laziness. Poverty falls in other ways like widowhood, aging, physical disability, natural disaster, or by any number of unforeseeable or insurmountable circumstances that cannot be broken by a more disciplined work habit (Acts 11:27–30). For these hurting saints, the church is called to remember them and love appropriately (Rom. 15:25–26; Gal. 2:10).

more stuff than his neighbor, is playing the sloth just as much as the man who stalls his vocation by wasting away his life on an Xbox (Eccles. 4:4–5). The sluggard and the workaholic both express self-centeredness. They both live out a desire to control their own lives. Neither lives to love. Neither lives to worship.

THE ZOMBIE

Sloth is buried in idleness and busyness, but the most common misconception about sloth is that it is desire-*less*. This is proven false on three counts. First, the *sluggard* is driven by desires:

> *The soul of the sluggard craves and gets nothing, while the soul of the diligent is richly supplied (Prov. 13:4).*

> *The desire of the sluggard kills him, for his hands refuse to labor. All day long he craves and craves (Prov. 21:25–26a).*

This desire to control life is a craving for selfish comfort, and it rots the soul. Second, the *workaholic* is likewise driven by desires:

> *"And others are the ones sown among thorns. They are those who hear the word, but the cares of the world and the deceitfulness of riches and the desires for other things enter in and choke the word, and it proves unfruitful"* (Mark 4:18–19).

Third, we meet the *zombie*. The zombie also lives a busy life, but does just enough to get things done, so he can get back to enjoying comfort. Comfort is what he craves. In order to get through his daily routine, his soul is Novocain numb. His daily routine becomes dead weight, for his soul is unable to see God (Luke 21:34–36).

"Sloth is not to be confused with laziness," warns Buechner of the zombie. "A slothful man may be a very busy man. He is a man who goes through the motions, who flies on automatic pilot. Like a man with a bad head cold, he has mostly lost his sense of taste and smell. He knows something's wrong with him, but not wrong enough to do anything about. Other people come and go, but through glazed eyes he hardly notices them. He is letting things run their course. He is getting through his life."[32]

Likewise, Richard John Neuhaus defines modern sloth as "evenings without number obliterated by television, evenings neither of entertainment nor of education, but of narcotized defense against time and duty." Above all else, he writes, sloth "is apathy, the refusal to engage the pathos of other lives and of God's life with them."[33]

The zombie is not driven by nothing, but has lost the desire to love and has lost the taste for what is truly satisfying. His eyes are glazed over on Sunday when it comes to matters of first importance. "The frozen, zombielike stares among many Sunday congregations is a sort of evidence of despair. And so also their roving eyes, their wandering minds," William Willamon laments. "We live in an age of a surfeit of distraction, of massive attention-deficit disorder. Failing to have our attention grabbed by anything of lasting value, our eyes, our minds wander, restlessly roving, failing to alight on

---

32   Frederick Buechner, *Wishful Thinking: A Theological ABC* (San Francisco: Harper & Row, 1973), 89–90.

33   Richard John Neuhaus, *Freedom for Ministry* (Grand Rapids: Eerdmans, 1992), 227.

anything worth having. And I'm no better than my congregation."[34]

True love is the fruit of a fervent, healthy soul (Rom. 12:10–11). But the zombie has grown dull of hearing, driven by a dead-eyed desire for something the world offers, impinged by daily life and the needs of others, manifested by a habitual addiction to distraction. This is the essence of the zombie's sloth.

SLOTH AND LEISURE

By poking a stick at these three kinds of sloth, we can wake up and shake off these tendencies in our own lives. The great paradox is that the sluggard who idolizes his free time, the workaholic who seeks self-constructed self-worth, and the zombie who sleepwalks through life, have all lost the capacity for true leisure.

In his book *Leisure: The Basis of Culture*, philosopher Josef Pieper argues that what draws all three types of sloth together is the desire to control life. "Leisure is not the attitude of mind of those who actively intervene, but of those who are open to everything; not of those who grab hold, but of those who leave the reins loose and who are free and easy themselves—almost like a man falling asleep."[35] In other words, the slothful desperately attempts to control his life in order to preserve comforts, dreading being interrupted by the needs of others. But he cannot respond to God's redirection. Life becomes self-centered and utilitarian. True leisure escapes the sloth.

---

34 William H. Willimon, *Sinning Like a Christian: A New Look at the 7 Deadly Sins* (Nashville: Abingdon Press, 2013), 85.
35 Josef Pieper, *Leisure: The Basis of Culture* (San Francisco: Ignatius Press, 2009), 47.

This failure to enjoy leisure is manifested in blindness to God's beauty. This is the picture Dante paints in his haunting descent into the *Inferno*. There he's led to the banks of a river made black by a stew of thick silt and mud. He looks down into the home of the submerged slothful, but there are no tortured bodies to see. Only the bubbling mud and gurgling voices rise to the surface. He listens close to hear the morbid hymn they sing: "'We were gloomy / in the sweet air made happy by the sun, / carrying within the smoke of sullenness. / Now we are smothered in the black slime.' This hymn they gurgle in their throats, for they cannot speak with whole words."[36] Forever the slothful lament this debauchery. In life, they could not love anyone but themselves; they are now forever unloved. They failed to find pleasure in the sweet clean air of creation; they are now bound to breathe mud. They failed to enjoy the sweet warmth of the sun on their skin; they are now submerged in dark slime. This is a profound statement about sloth. Sloth, at its core, is a lack of appetite for God's gifts. Sloth is a blindness and deadness to God's beauty. Sloth is the incapacity for true leisure.

The sluggard defends his comforts and grows blind to the beauty of God. The workaholic clutches his salary, his power, and his image, and loses the leisure he needs to flourish as a creature before God. The zombie sees life as a series of compounded distractions, gets buried in the details, feeds off candies of diversion, and slowly dozes off into a spiritual coma. True leisure and true joy in God has escaped them all. They are lazy-souled, and as Thomas Manton says: "Everlasting joys will not drop into the mouth of the lazy soul; these things are not trifles, they will cost us diligence and se-

---

36 *Inferno: The Comedy of Dante Alighieri*, edited by Dante Alighieri and Tom Simone (Newburyport: Focus, 2006), 70.

riousness" (Phil. 2:12; Heb. 11:6).[37] All three forms of sloth are boredom with God, and doomed to death. Sloth kills.

IN THE WORLD, FOR THE CHURCH, FROM THE HEART

This trio of sloth—sluggard, workaholic, zombie—rattles the cage of our preexisting assumptions. So maybe the best way to illustrate sloth is to show what sloth *is not*. Whether or not he intended it, in 1 Thessalonians 4, Paul confronts sloth in all three expressions.

The slothful misunderstand that every one of God's creatures are created to thrive in one or more environments. This is obvious in the animal world, and just as true of God's image-bearers. And so the opposite of a slothful life is a holistic life flourishing in three balanced environments: (1) my routine before the world, (2) my mission for the church, and (3) my enchantment with God. We work in the world, for the church, and from the heart.

Environment 1: My Routine before the World (1 Thess. 4:11–12)

God really cares about our 9-to-5. He wants us to show up to work on time, to work full days, and to keep our homes in order. Our daily routines and the maintenance of our houses are visible to others—a quiet, faithful life making a bold testimony to God's worth. The purpose of our daily work is not to protect our comforts, but to support God's work in the church. This message of diligence and routine undoes the sluggard.

37 Thomas Manton, *The Complete Works of Thomas Manton* (London: James Nisbet & Co., 1873), 11:458.

Environment 2: My Mission for the Church (4:9–10)

For the church to flourish, it must have members who are financially independent. The local church needs financial support in order to advance missions in the region, country, and world. The sluggard, the workaholic, and the zombie all have in common a lack of love. Sloth is lazy love.[38] They see needs as interruptions, not opportunities. Paul reminds every Christian that our fraternal love for the church (local, regional, and global) comes when we first master our daily routines, and then apply the fruit to the needs of others. When ordinary Christians are financially independent and domestically in order, their talents and time are available to serve the local and global church.

Environment 3: My Enchantment with God (4:13–18)

But there is one more environment where the Christian must avoid sloth: the cosmic one, the environment outside and above the others. Even more than our routine before the world, or our mission for the church, we are called to build our delight in God. We are created to live in awe of unseen realities. We hope and trust in an unseen Savior. We trust in his resurrection from the dead and his future return. We trust that our bodies will be resurrected from the dead. We put all our eternal hope into Christ, which means we live in this world as though we were in an enchanted story. It's not enough to work hard 9-to-5, raise a few children, mow the lawn, care for our church family, and serve the lost; we must do all this as Christians with a living hope and a God-centered delight in what we cannot see.

---

38   Rebecca DeYoung, *Glittering Vices: A New Look at the Seven Deadly Sins and Their Remedies* (Grand Rapids: Brazos, 2009), 79–98.

The death of sloth is a living awareness that we are caught up into God's plan, and barreling along in history that is out of our control, and without full knowledge of where everything is headed. But we know, in Christ, it's going to be wonderful. So we hold the reins loosely; we don't go through the motions of life like zombies; we trust God and love every step.

SLAYING THE THREE-HEADED SLOTH

1 Thessalonians 4 exposes each manifestation of sloth by revealing what it means to thrive in three environments concurrently.

SLOTH PERSON	ENVIRONMENT	APATHY WITH
Sluggard	Local Routine	Neighbor
Workaholic	Global Mission	Church
Zombie	Cosmic Enchantment	God

The slothful sluggard is confronted by a calling for diligence in daily routines. The slothful workaholic is confronted by an investment in love for other Christians in the church. The slothful zombie is confronted by true enchantment with God, to awaken to the glory of union with Christ and the cosmic-sized work of God in the gospel.

In a sense, the most relevant confrontation with sloth is found in the local church. The gates of sloth shall not overcome her. Our church gatherings themselves are part of our glorious routine, if done right.[39] In community, as we gath-

---

39 Sloth makes a mess of the local church by opening the door to envy and other sins. "Among the seven deadly sins of medieval lore was sloth (acedia)—a state of hard-bitten, joyless apathy of spirit. There is a lot of it around today in Christian circles; the symptoms are personal spiritual

er to celebrate, the sloth finds his true leisure.[40] We gather
to love and support other believers, those in our region and
around the world. There we marvel together with enchantment at our God. We rejoice in the incarnation, life, death,
and resurrection of our Savior, and voice our longing together
for his return and for the resurrection of our bodies, when
we'll see and experience him with all the more clarity and intensity.

The local church is a hard sell for the slothful—but what
makes it a hard sell also makes it good medicine for the sluggard, the workaholic, and the zombie within. We put off sloth
to live out this holistic life, to flourish as routine people, as
missional people, and as eschatological people—growing in
hope and love and joy in God.

inertia combined with critical cynicism about the churches and supercil-
ious resentment of other Christians' initiative and enterprise." J. I. Packer,
Knowing God (Downers Grove: InterVarsity Press, 1993), 106.
40   The ultimate point of Pieper in *Leisure*.

6

GREED

DAVID MATHIS

"Take care, and be on your guard against all covetousness,
for one's life does not consist in the abundance of possessions."
—Jesus (Luke 12:15)

Greed is good. So says Gordon Gekko, one of Hollywood's most memorable villains, played by Michael Douglas in the 1987 film *Wall Street*. Greed has long been "the hobgoblin of capitalism,"[41] the vice that moves the Invisible Hand of the free market. Economist Adam Smith would suggest we call it by sweeter names. After Smith, Alfred Marshall went so far as to defend "the love of money"—the precise thing the New Testament so clearly condemns in 1 Timothy 6:10 and Hebrews 13:5—provided its motive is one of "many of the highest, the most refined, and the most unselfish elements of our nature."

We are awash today in greed. It meets us at nearly every turn, beckons us from almost every advertisement, is woven into the fabric of regular interaction, and diabolically remains so inconspicuous. It gnaws at the uneasy conscience of our

---

41   John Paul Rollert, "Greed Is Good: A 300-Year History of a Dangerous Idea" in *The Atlantic*, 7 April 2014. Available online at http://www.theatlantic.com/business/archive/2014/04/greed-is-good-a-300-year-history-of-a-dangerous-idea/360265.

finances, as we openly acknowledge its ugliness when unrestrained, but benefit from its unintended effects "for the public good." We might gasp when we catch greed red-handed, but typically it's so careful to stay out of sight, where it breeds and multiplies, evasive and pervasive. Our society, by some common grace, may condemn greed in theory, but we're slow to point a finger at specifics, especially when the finger might land on us. As John Paul Rollert writes,

> If we reject some conduct but rarely admit an example, we enjoy the benefit of being high-minded without the burden of moral restraint. We also embolden that behavior, which proceeds with a presumptive blessing. As a matter of public discourse and polite conversation, "Greed" is unlikely to be "Good" anytime soon, but a vice need not become a virtue for the end result to look the same.[42]

We may not formally baptize unrestrained greed, but we have winked at it a thousand times, and swallowed our reservations. And the weed happily grows to fill every inch we give it.

IN THE BIBLE AND IN US

American capitalism is not the origin of greed, though. It is frequently warned against in the Bible, and for more than 1,500 years, the church has recognized greed as one of the seven deadly sins. Modern fiction may have given us Gordon Gekko and Ebenezer Scrooge, but the Bible has Gehazi, Elijah's greedy assistant (2 Kings 5:20–27), and the rich fool planning for bigger barns (Luke 12:16–21). Most haunting of all is Judas Iscariot, who for thirty pieces of silver betrayed

42 Ibid.

not only his mentor and friend, but God himself in human flesh.

Deep down, we know greed all too well. It lurks in the hearts of rich and poor, in the vilest offender and the professing believer. In our own soul, we have felt the voracious appetite Aquinas calls "the desire for profit which knows no limit." We've experienced the tug of greed which "never has enough" (Hab. 2:5), and we live in a society that, perhaps as much as any other, is an unrivaled community of "hearts trained in greed" (2 Pet. 2:14).

We may think of it in euphemisms and call it by pet names like consumerism or hoarding or extreme couponing or simply "saving up for the future," but we feel its intense pull when contemplating a gift, walking store aisles, flipping though a catalogue, passing a billboard, watching ads online and on television, and considering how much to tip the waitress. It's a nasty weed that has taken root not only "out there" in our society and among our acquaintances, but "in here," in our churches, in our own families, and in our own hearts. But before we start hacking away at the kudzu, we need to look at greed's nature and schemes—how deep the root goes—and what specific weapons wield the strongest power.

GOOD DESIRE GONE WRONG

Greed, known as "avarice" among the ancients, is the inordinate desire for wealth and possessions. It is "an excessive love," according to Rebecca DeYoung, "for money or any possession that money can buy."[43] Biblically, greed is largely synonymous with "covetousness," which typically craves things or possessions. This covetousness is the last thing expressly forbidden in the Ten Commandments (Ex. 20:17, "You shall not covet"),

---

43   Rebecca DeYoung, *Glittering Vices: A New Look at the Seven Deadly Sins and Their Remedies* (Grand Rapids: Brazos, 2009), 100.

communicating some of the grave seriousness of greed. Elsewhere, greed surfaces as "the desire to be rich" (1 Tim. 6:9).
Just a verse later, it's "the love of money" (also Heb. 13:5) which
"is a root of all kinds of evils" (1 Tim. 6:10). Another example
is the laying up of treasures on earth, which is set against laying up treasures in heaven (Matt. 6:19).

While these manifestations of greed, in the Bible and in
our lives, are so concretely material, it's important to note that
greed is an inordinate *desire*, a disordered *love*, a revolt in the
heart, a misplaced *craving* (as in 1 Tim. 6:10). "From within,
out of the heart," says Jesus, "come evil thoughts, sexual im-
morality, theft, murder, adultery, *coveting*, wickedness, deceit,
sensuality, envy, slander, pride, foolishness" (Mark 7:21–22).

Greed is a good desire gone wrong. God created human-
ity—vice-regents in his lavish creation—to have and possess,
with a healthy desire to acquire. To covet means to desire
some object we shouldn't, or to desire it with an inappropriate
intensity. The desire for possession itself is not evil, but good.
The desiring God designed us to be desiring humans, and one
day have all our good desires met. But when desire is out of
proportion or misdirected, it is sin—the very essence of sin.

In this way, greed cuts both ways. It is not just a sin that
stalks those who have and selfishly keep, but also those who
have not. Scripture, writes Brian Hedges, "locates the problem of greed in the inordinate affections of our hearts, rather
than in money or possessions *per se*. This means you can have
a greed problem, even if you don't have a lot of money. The issue is not what you possess, but what possesses you."[44] Greed
plagues the prodigal and the penny-pincher alike.

44   Brian Hedges, *Hit List: Taking Aim at the Seven Deadly Sins* (Minneapolis: Cruciform Press, 2014), Kindle locations 1047–1049.

GRIEVOUS, DEADLY, DARK LORD

What possesses us has something profound to say about God, even when we we're blind to our bondage. In giving ground to greed, we fall under the condemnation of Jeremiah 2:13, "My people have forsaken me, the fountain of living waters, and hewed out cisterns for themselves, broken cisterns that can hold no water." Greed dishonors God by saying that we don't find him trustworthy to provide for us. Instead, we store up, trying to over-provide for ourselves. Greed also says we don't think God and his provisions are enough to satisfy the desires of our souls. Instead, we feed our appetites with things—more things, expensive things, new things.

Greed is idolatry (Col. 3:5; Eph. 5:5). It is unbelief in the heart directed toward money and possessions. We don't believe God and his goods are enough, so we turn elsewhere, and thus "the contentment that the heart should be getting from God," writes John Piper, greed "starts to get from something else."[45] Greed makes a god of something other than God—which means it is not only a breach of the tenth commandment, but also the first (Ex. 20:3).

Greed, then, is no small indiscretion and innocent vice. It is an assault on the one who designed our good desires, an attack on the good, providing God of the universe. He says, "Open your mouth wide, and I will fill it" (Ps. 81:10), but greed stoops and takes a mouthful of dirt. Greed chokes and starves saving faith (Mark 4:19), and so Jesus says, without mincing any words, "You cannot serve God and money" (Matt. 6:24). If the professing believer is unrepentant, greed is a disciplinable offense in the church (1 Cor. 5:11). Leaders must not be known as "lovers of money" or "greedy for gain" (1 Tim. 3:3, 8; Titus 1:7; 1 Pet. 5:2). We may expect the world to be greedy,

45 John Piper, *Future Grace: The Purifying Power of the Promises of God*, 2nd edition (Colorado Springs: Multnomah, 2012), 221.

but not the Bride (Eph. 5:3). And yet we feel the burning embers of greed in our own hearts.

Because greed is a forsaking of our good design, and an affront to our Creator, there must be consequences. God's reputation is at stake, as well as the joy of his children. It is fitting that God's righteous wrath come upon those who neglect and demean him, the supremely valuable one. "Because of these things," including covetousness, "the wrath of God comes upon the sons of disobedience" (Eph. 5:6; Col. 3:5–6). Greed is deadly because, like all sin, its wages are death (Rom. 3:23). Left unchecked, unfought, and free to grow and deepen and expand, it leads not just to devastating relational and financial consequences in this life, but eternal death (James 1:14–15). Indeed, the greedy will not and cannot inherit the kingdom of God (1 Cor. 6:10).

A second reason greed is deadly is that it brings an army of destruction in its wake. She is the mother of more wickedness. Greed not only blocks love (Rom. 13:9–10; 1 John 3:17), but breeds death. She gives birth to lying (2 Pet. 2:3), strife (Prov. 28:25), fighting, quarreling, and even murder (Jam. 4:2). "The love of money is a root of all kinds of evils" (1 Tim. 6:10). "The kind of heart that finds contentment in money and not in God," explains Piper, "is the kind of heart that produces all other kinds of evils."[46] Billy Graham goes so far as to say that greed "is probably the parent of more evil than all the other sins."[47] And so, we must "put to death . . . covetousness" (Col. 3:5) before it deals its deathblow to our souls.

MOUNTING THE FIGHT

The war on greed is a lifelong campaign. Victory doesn't happen with a single choice or one dramatic action. There may

46   Ibid., 225.
47   Quoted in Hedges, *Hit List*.

be signal triumphs in which large tracts of our hearts are re-turned to their rightful owner. We should expect some loss-es, but hopefully more gains. We will be prey to some of the worst guerilla warfare, as greed often attacks when we least expect it. But he who began a good work in us promises to complete it, even as he also promises not to add the finishing touches "until the day of Christ" (Phil. 1:6).

For this war, as with any war, we will need offensive and defensive tactics. The task of defense is to recognize greed in its camouflage and confront it. It means sniffing it out when it's hiding in the brush, seeing its subtle footprints on the path—not mainly in the lives of our neighbors, but in our own hearts. The grace of God in the gospel not only *forgives* our disordered desires and actions, but *trains* us "to renounce ungodliness and worldly passions" (Titus 2:11–12). The grace of God teaches us to increasingly recognize the tentacles of greed in our lives, and when we do, to renounce them. To smoke them out, we can ask ourselves some simple questions: Is my spending marked by Christian generosity? What does the use of my money say about what makes me most happy? Am I collecting for this life? Is my spending explicitly sup-porting the spread of the gospel and the needs of the church? From a different angle, is my spending so cautious that it keeps me from loving those close to me well?

But defense alone will not win the war. We must go on the offensive. The goal is not just to keep ourselves from greed—to say *no* to its lies—but to give ourselves more fully in love to its opposites. Greed holds out the promise of plea-sure in some illicit desire. It whispers, *If I only had that as well, then I'd be happy*. But in Christ, we not only renounce sin, but we strike with the power of a superior pleasure. We "make every effort to supplement [our] faith with virtue, and virtue with knowledge" (2 Pet. 1:5), we both strengthen our defenses against greed, and march offensively on the gates of hell.

Beware, though, of simplistic conceptions of greed's enemies. The opposite of greed is not asceticism—forsaking the
goodness of creation. Rather, the heart of greed's discontent is
countered with a deeper, fuller, richer contentment in Christ.

CONTENTMENT IN CHRIST

Faith takes the frontline in the assault against greed, target-
ing it at its root of unbelief—in particular, faith as contentment in Christ, faith that is seeking its ultimate satisfaction
in God. Such faith—such contentment in Christ—is greed's
great nemesis. In *The Rare Jewel of Christian Contentment*, Jeremiah Burroughs defines contentment as "that sweet, inward,
gracious frame of spirit, which freely submits to and delights
in God's wise and fatherly disposal in every condition."[48] In
other words, contentment is sustained faith that inwardly
steadies us during changing and trying circumstances. Three
texts paint this definition in greater detail.

1) The Secret Is Christ

First is Paul's stunning testimony in Philippians 4:11–13:

> *I have learned in whatever situation I am to be content. I*
> *know how to be brought low, and I know how to abound.*
> *In any and every circumstance, I have learned the secret*
> *of facing plenty and hunger, abundance and need. I can*
> *do all things through him who strengthens me.*

The apostle was genuinely grateful to receive financial support from the Philippians, but his contentment in Christ
guards him against greed. His good desire for supplies and

---

48   Jeremiah Burroughs, *The Rare Jewel of Christian Contentment* (Banner
of Truth, 1964), 19. Quoted in Hedges, *Hit List.*

sufficient income is protected from sinful disorder by his steadying contentment in Christ. He calls it "the secret" of contentment: that inner stability that comes from knowing Jesus as the rewarder of those who seek him (Heb. 11:6), and that he himself is the reward of surpassing value (Phil. 3:7–8).

2) The Fight Is for Faith

Next is 1 Timothy 6:6–10, casting contentment in Christ as the opposite of greed and "the love of money":

> [G]odliness with contentment is great gain, for we brought nothing into the world, and we cannot take anything out of the world. But if we have food and clothing, with these we will be content. But those who desire to be rich fall into temptation, into a snare, into many senseless and harmful desires that plunge people into ruin and destruction. For the love of money is a root of all kinds of evils. It is through this craving that some have wandered away from the faith and pierced themselves with many pangs.

Again, we have a good desire for the basic needs of life: "if we have food and clothing, with these we will be content." But beyond them, Paul warns of "the love of money" and the "desire to be rich." Again, it is not that wealth and money are evils in themselves. Rather, the evil is in our hearts, in disordered desire and inordinate love for the riches.

Where then does the battle against greed begin? We counter the unbelief of greed with contentment in Christ. Such faith sees Jesus not only as true, but as beautiful and good. Greed's foil is faith in Christ as our Provision. Paul warns against greed, then immediately says, "As for you, O man of God, flee these things. Pursue righteousness, godliness, faith, love, steadfastness, gentleness. Fight the good fight of the *faith*" (1 Tim. 6:11–12).

3) The Promise Is the Power

The third clear text on contentment, and perhaps the most powerful, is Hebrews 13:5:

> Keep your life free from love of money, and be content with what you have, for he has said, "I will never leave you nor forsake you."

Greed not only flows from the lie that God is not enough for us in the present, but the fear that he will not adequately provide for our future. Greed not only wants to hoard, acquire, and possess more today, but it also fears that God will not meet our sense of need and be enough for us tomorrow. Hebrews 13:5 not only teaches us that the opposite of the "love of money" is being "content with what you have," but it also takes God's stunning promise of provision to Joshua (Josh. 1:5) and gives it to every Christian: "I will never leave you nor forsake you." Far better than having some seemingly endless, but finite reserve of possessions is having the infinite God himself and his truly endless energy and resourcefulness to supply our every need, and to lavish his grace on us "far more abundantly than all that we ask or think" (Eph. 3:20).

COMPASSION, GENEROSITY, AND SACRIFICE

Having severed the root of greed through such contentment in Christ, we are increasingly freed for the full flowering of love in its stead. Liberated from greed and our slavery to its cravings, we're freed to develop an eye and heart for others (compassion), and to give of ourselves to meet their needs (generosity), even when it costs us our own possessions (sacrifice). In doing so, we build the siegeworks for our lifelong attack on greed.

Hebrews 10:32–34 gives us a glimpse into how it works, and verse 34 may be the most pointed text in all the Bible for the heart of the battle.

> *Recall the former days when, after you were enlightened, you endured a hard struggle with sufferings, 33 sometimes being publicly exposed to reproach and affliction, and sometimes being partners with those so treated. 34 For you had compassion on those in prison, and you joyfully accepted the plundering of your property, since you knew that you yourselves had a better possession and an abiding one.*

Verse 34 speaks to the compassion that arose in these young believers who, content in Christ and liberated from greed, *joyfully* embrace the sacrifice of their possessions. Then we get the great reason: "you knew that you yourselves had a better possession and an abiding one." They had something greater and more durable than everything else they had. We have finally landed at ground zero in the war. This is the key: conquering greed with the specific superior pleasure of having Christ as our possession.

Content in Christ, these persecuted Christians were free from the disordered desire to guard their precious earthly possessions. They were free because they knew that they had a possession that far exceeded every other and that could not be taken away. Jesus, their better and abiding possession, had begun to meet every good desire in their souls for possession. He was the Treasure that made it possible to lose every other treasure. Knowing the pleasure of having Christ released their grasp on their lowercase, plural *possessions*—and whatever pleasures they may bring—because by faith they had an uppercase, singular *Possession*. And so not only was selfish greed destroyed at the root, but the seed of faith, planted in its place, grew and stretched and flowered into selfless compassion, generosity, and sacrifice.

A REAL, BUT RELATIVE STANDARD

Each of us must wrestle personally with the fine line between healthy and unhealthy desires for possessions. Augustine offers a standard by pointing to "the needs of this life," by which he means, says DeYoung,

> . . . not just what is necessary for bare subsistence, but also what is necessary for living a life "becoming" or appropriate to human beings. The point is not to live on crusts of bread with bare walls and threadbare clothes. The point is that a fully human life is lived in a way free from being enslaved to our stuff. Our possessions are meant to serve our needs and our humanness, rather than our lives being centered around service to our possessions and our desires for them.[49]

Discerning what is and is not "a fully human life . . . free from being enslaved to our stuff" will vary from place to place and person to person. God simply means for us to embrace the truth that, "Each one must give as he has decided in his heart, not reluctantly or under compulsion, for God loves a cheerful giver" (2 Cor. 9:7). While it might be unwise to prescribe particulars here, it can be helpful to create general categories, and to describe errors to avoid.

One thing to note is that human life is not a static existence. God made us for rhythms and cadences, for feasting

---

49 *Glittering Vices*, 106.

and fasting. There is benefit, even if minimal, in identifying and naming the extremes of sustained opulence, on the one hand, and austerity, on the other. We need a place for both financial feasting and fasting. We should abhor the so-called prosperity gospel, and not be fooled by loveless stinginess masquerading as Christian stewardship. However, while discerning from person to person precisely what's too little or too much is no easy task, Piper wisely observes, "The impossibility of drawing a line between night and day doesn't mean you can't know it's midnight."[50]

A final thing we might note here in terms of a practical standard is the test of sacrifice. Do you ever abstain from fulfilling your own sense of need in order to give to others? A life without the practice of sacrifice—a love that suffers want to meet the needs of others—is not a fully Christian life.

MY GREAT POSSESSION

It is in sacrifice that our lives echo in some faint way that one decisive event that secured our every advance against greed. The triumph was won long before we came onto the scene. Greed received its own deathblow when the Son of God himself came ashore and fortified the beachhead. The one who possessed everything made himself nothing that we might have everything in him. He didn't grasp at his infinite wealth, but opened his hand and emptied himself (Phil. 2:6–7). "Though he was rich, yet for your sake he became poor, so that you by his poverty might become rich" (2 Cor. 8:9). He was obedient to death, even death on a cross (Phil. 2:8), robbed of all he had, including his garment and his dignity, and even stripped of his communion with the Father, crying

50   Collin Hansen, "Piper on Pastors' Pay," The Gospel Coalition, 6 November 2013, http://www.thegospelcoalition.org/article/piper-on-pastors-pay.

out, "My God, my God, why have you forsaken me?" (Matt. 27:46). Then he rose again over greed, death, and hell, and is preparing, for those whom he possesses, a new creation in which they will own it all (1 Cor. 3:21; Matt. 5:5). We will share in the divine inheritance and possess the whole world.

And so, having the abundant grace of God, we cry out against greed, *Jesus is my Great Possession*. He is my better possession and abiding one (Heb. 10:34). He is the one whose presence is the great promise that severs for me the power of the love of money (Heb. 13:5). He is my treasure hidden in the field, for whom I would gladly sell all I had (Matt. 13:44).

As I walk past the window display, or contemplate some generous act, or ponder purchasing that new device, the deepest solution to my inordinate desire to have more and more is not to have nothing, but to have Christ. The great remedy to greed's disordered love is the daily reordering of my heart in view of my Beloved. The death knell of greed is the simple refrain of Solomon's Song: "I am my beloved's, and he is mine" (Song 2:16; 6:3; 7:10). All I have—and ever could truly want to possess—is summed up in Christ and his provision.

7

GLUTTONY

JOHNATHON BOWERS

Oh, gluttony, full of cursedness!
Oh first cause of our ruination!
Oh origin of our damnation,
Until Christ had bought us with his blood again!
—Geoffrey Chaucer, "The Pardoner's Tale"[51]

Food has been with us since the beginning. In fact, diet was one of the first things God addressed with Adam and Eve in the Garden. "Behold, I have given you every plant yielding seed that is on the face of all the earth, and every tree with seed in its fruit. You shall have them for food" (Gen. 1:29). As part of God's good creation, food reminds us that we are not self-sufficient, that we depend on something outside of us for our life. Food can heal. Food can sustain. But as we see in Genesis 2–3, food can also kill. After planting the man in the garden, God instructed him to eat from every tree—with one exception: the tree of the knowledge of good and evil. "[F]or," said God, "in the day that you eat of it you shall surely die" (Gen. 2:17). Tragically, Adam and Eve chose death over life in response to the serpent's scheme. And life and food have never been the same.

---

51   Geoffrey Chaucer, *The Canterbury Tales*, trans. Peter Tuttle; Barnes & Noble Classics (New York: Barnes & Noble, 2007), 495.

As we consider the deadly sin of gluttony, it's significant that the fall of mankind played itself out in the first couple's palates. The temptation was all about the appetite. Our fall from grace could have involved a murder, as with Cain and Abel. It could have involved rape or incest or any other wicked act. But instead, the fate of mankind was bound up with a snack. Why?

In Genesis 3:6 we see that the fruit represented much more than sustenance for Eve: "So when the woman saw that the tree was good for food, and that it was a delight to the eyes, and that the tree was to be desired to make one wise, she took of its fruit and ate, and she also gave some to her husband who was with her, and he ate." In the moment of temptation, the fruit embodied Eve's deepest cravings: cravings for pleasure, for beauty, for wisdom. Rather than satisfy these cravings within the boundaries of God's good design, Eve opened her mouth — and her heart — to rebellion.

WHAT IS GLUTTONY?

Put concisely, gluttony is food worship. It directs the appetite toward improper ends, looking to our taste buds for the satisfaction that God offers us in his fellowship through Christ. Now, many define gluttony as overeating. While gluttony often produces overeating, I hesitate to call overeating gluttony's essence for several reasons. First, reducing gluttony to overeating can create a false sense of guilt over occasional feasting. At times, enjoying lots of food can be a means of delighting in God's goodness. For example, under the Mosaic law the Israelites were expected to devote a tenth of their grain, wine, and oil to the Lord each year by eating it in his presence at the tabernacle (Deut. 14:22–23). If they lived far from the tabernacle, they could sell their tithe and bring the money with them on their pilgrimage. Once they finished their journey, they were to convert the money back into food and feast before the Lord: "[S]pend the money," God instructed, "for whatever you desire — oxen or sheep or wine or strong drink, whatever your appetite craves. And you shall eat there before the Lord your God and rejoice, you and your household" (Deut. 14:26). God does not begrudge a good feast from time to time, so we should be careful, as we define gluttony, to allow space for larger-than-normal, celebratory meals.

Second, equating gluttony with overeating can minimize the role that our desires play in our decisions. Remember that Eve ate the forbidden fruit because it appealed to her longing for pleasure, beauty, and wisdom. With gluttony, we look to food to satisfy some deeper craving, whether for comfort, for purpose, or for a sense of control. For this reason, it won't do when addressing gluttony to say we should simply will ourselves to eat less. We need to pay close attention to our desires as well. Augustine, for example, wrote in his *Confessions*, "It is no uncleanness in food that I fear, but the uncleanness of greed."[52]

Finally, our definition of gluttony needs to go beyond mere overeating to incorporate another form of food abuse: snootiness. It's possible to seek our satisfaction in the food we consume. It's also possible — and just as dangerous — to seek our satisfaction in the food we avoid. In *The Screwtape Letters*, C. S. Lewis — through the mouth of the demon Screwtape — labeled both responses to food as gluttony. The first he called the gluttony of excess; the second, the gluttony of delicacy. In the excerpt below, Screwtape writes to his nephew Wormwood, explaining the situation of a woman whose discriminating palate makes life difficult for those around her:

---

52 Augustine, *The Confessions*, trans. Maria Boulding; Vintage Spiritual Classics (New York: Vintage, 1998), 227.

> *She is a positive terror to hostesses and servants. She is always turning from what has been offered her to say with a demure little sigh and a smile 'Oh please, please… all I want is a cup of tea, weak but not too weak, and the teeniest weeniest bit of really crisp toast.' You see? Because what she wants is smaller and less costly than what has been set before her, she never recognises as gluttony her determination to get what she wants, however troublesome it may be to others. At the very moment of indulging her appetite she believes that she is practising temperance.*[53]

In this example, the woman is a slave to her stomach, but she has deceived herself into thinking she is free. She is an undercover glutton, hiding her guilt even from herself. How many of us might fall into this category? Obsessing over a particular diet, anxiously counting calories, disdaining certain foods as morally suspect: it's all a variation on the same idolatrous theme.[54] Food has become a god.

Gluttony, therefore, is food worship displayed both in excessive eating and in pharisaical avoidance. While it would be beneficial to consider both manifestations of gluttony in this chapter, for the sake of space I will limit my focus to excessive eating. It's important, however, to remember that since both kinds of gluttony involve the worship of food, the biblical remedy to one is necessarily bound up with the biblical rem-

---

53　C. S. Lewis, *The Screwtape Letters* (New York: HarperCollins, 2001), 87–88. Italics original.

54　To clarify, I'm not talking here about those with food allergies or other medical conditions that require special dietary restrictions. Instead, I'm talking about those who feel an unhealthy need to achieve a certain body image or who have been unduly influenced by the many popular jeremiads against gluten, refined sugar, or non-organic products.

edy to the other. With this in mind, let's consider the dangers of gluttony.

Danger #1: Belittling God

In Philippians 3, Paul warns his readers about those who "walk as enemies of the cross of Christ" (3:18). "Their end is destruction," he continues, *"their god is their belly,* and they glory in their shame, with minds set on earthly things" (3:19, emphasis added). This text identifies the first and primary danger of gluttony: it puts food in the place of God. Gluttony presents the chief end of man as a table well-stocked and a stomach well-filled. Hunger becomes the great enemy; the refrigerator then stands as the temple where we find our deliverance.

Gluttony, like all sin, distorts the purpose of God's good creation. Food was never meant to be an end in itself. It is a means of receiving needed nourishment and a sign pointing us to our need for God. The rhythm of hunger and satisfaction we experience in our stomach is a dramatization of the relationship between God and our very existence. This is the point of God's word to Israel in Deuteronomy 8:3: "[M]an does not live by bread alone, but man lives by every word that comes from the mouth of the Lord." By treating food as an end in itself, gluttony ruins our appetite for fellowship with our Creator. It exchanges the glory of the immortal God for a ham sandwich and kettle chips.

For this reason, what's at stake in the fight against gluttony is not primarily an ever-expanding waistline. Eternal life is at stake. James condemns the rich who "have lived on the earth in luxury and in self-indulgence." Why? Because through such abandonment to the passions of their flesh, they had "fattened [their] hearts in a day of slaughter" (James 5:5). And beyond warranting the judgment to come, gluttony is itself a present experience of that very judgment. In 1 Timothy 5, Paul explains the qualifications for widows who should receive the church's financial support. He warns against supporting a widow who is known for self-indulgence, for, he writes, "she who is self-indulgent is dead even while she lives" (5:6). Because true life consists in feasting on the words of God, to live as though bread alone sustains us is the spiritual equivalent of gnawing on the wind.

Danger #2: Hating Our Brother

A second danger of gluttony is the damage it causes in our relationships. Gluttony is often tied with injustice. When a person consumes more food than he ought to in certain contexts, someone else may be going hungry. Our appetites have social consequences. This was the case with the rich man and Lazarus. "There was a rich man," Jesus tells the Pharisees, "who was clothed in purple and fine linen and who feasted sumptuously every day" (Luke 16:19). By all accounts, this man was a glutton. Occasional feasting is appropriate, as we've seen already. But the rich man feasted sumptuously. And not just on weekends or government holidays, but every day. This man ate like a king, like the god of his own universe. But what compounded his transgression was his corresponding neglect of Lazarus. Jesus continues, "And at his gate was laid a poor man named Lazarus, covered with sores, who desired to be fed with what fell from the rich man's table" (Luke 16:20–21). The use of the phrase "desired to be fed" suggests that this desire was never satisfied. Unlike the crippled Mephibosheth, whom David invited to share in his royal feasting (2 Sam. 9:1–13), Lazarus spent his days cut off from the rich pseudo-king's abundance.

Gluttony insists on the satisfaction of our bodily cravings, even if someone else has to go hungry as a result. Personally,

I see it most clearly in my own heart during group dinners, especially when only a limited amount of food is available. In my worst moments, I'll tremble at the thought of eating less than I'm used to. Instead of loving my brother by making sure he has enough to eat, I'll help myself to a nice "me" portion, knowing full well that I've cheated those coming after me. Whether they ever know that I have slighted them or not, the sinful state of my heart is real. Others are not loved and God is not glorified. The Corinthian church faced a similar problem. When they came together for the Lord's Supper, some got drunk while others went hungry (1 Cor. 11:21). Inequity is the currency of gluttony. When we yield to this sin, we consent to the poisonous fruit it bears in our relationships.

Danger #3: Self-Indulgence

Finally, gluttony is dangerous because it is a form of self-indulgence, and self-indulgence is a rolling stone. Never content to settle down with our sweet tooth and maybe have a couple kids, it's always itching to travel, to meet foreign vices in lands beyond the sea. If we abandon ourselves to whatever our stomachs crave, we shouldn't be surprised to find other sinful indulgences in our lives as well. Consider Hophni and Phinehas as an example. These two men were sons of Eli the priest. Although they ministered in the house of the Lord at Shiloh, 1 Samuel 2:12 makes it clear that they were unbelievers, "worthless men" in fact. Whenever an Israelite would come to offer sacrifice, Hophni and Phinehas would help themselves to generous portions of the meat, threatening with violence anyone who stood in their way (1 Sam. 2:13–16). The text ends, "Thus the sin of the young men was very great in the sight of the Lord, for the men treated the offering of the Lord with contempt" (1 Sam. 2:17).

In their disordered hunger, Hophni and Phinehas both belittled God and wronged other people. But notice how their lack of restraint infected their sexuality as well. Several verses later in 1 Samuel 2, we read that Eli's sons "lay with the women who were serving at the tent of meeting" (2:22). Don't miss the connection here. Gluttony and sexual perversion may seem like independent evils, but they both draw their strength from the same dark source: self-indulgence. To mix the metaphor, self-indulgence is a chameleon. Put it near food and it shades itself like gluttony. Put it near a pretty woman (or a smooth-talking man) and it takes on the colors of lust. Because of this, we cannot afford to think that our eating habits are somehow neutral territory in the fight against sin. If we make peace with gluttony, we will make peace — in one form or another — with other vices.

STRATEGIES FOR THE FIGHT

Thankfully, there's another option. We can make war on gluttony, strengthened by the hope that any progress here will bear fruit in surprising ways elsewhere. How, though, do we fight gluttony? Here are ten suggestions.

1) Remember that self-control is freedom and gluttony is bondage.

Gluttony often tempts us into believing that restraining our impulses is oppressive and limiting. But like all righteous boundaries, self-control creates the space for our flourishing under God. The glutton does not truly enjoy food. He is imprisoned by it.

2) Remember that self-control is a gift of God, not a result of self-reliant willpower.

I don't mean to suggest that we should pray for self-control and then do nothing until it shows up. Self-control is a discipline. But we work only because God is at work in us first (Phil. 2:12–13). Speaking of gluttony, Augustine writes, "[S]ometimes it creeps up on your servant, and only your mercy will drive it away. For no one can be continent except by your gift."[55] Only by God's enablement can we rule our appetites as we ought.

3) Remember that Christ has atoned for our gluttony and given us a spirit of self-control.

Christ, the very embodiment of self-control, was vilified as a glutton and a drunkard (Matt. 11:19; Luke 7:34), and this because he loved sharing meals with sinners. He took on the reproach of the sinners' table so that we—gluttons and louts all—might know the joy of the Lord's table. Jesus has cleansed us of our disordered cravings. In him, we have crucified the flesh with its passions and desires (Gal. 5:24). What's more, Christ has sent his Spirit to fill us, the Spirit who bears the fruit of self-control in his people (Gal. 5:22).

4) Glut yourself on Jesus.

Jesus is the true Bread that has come down from heaven (John 6:32). And this bread has no recommended serving size. We can—and must—eat all we want, and come back for seconds. In the words of Jonathan Edwards, "There is no such

---

55   Augustine, *The Confessions*, 226.

thing as excess in our taking of . . . spiritual food. There is no such virtue as temperance in spiritual feasting."[56]

5) *View the Lord's Table as a training ground for self-control.*

Whenever we eat the bread and drink the cup, we make war on gluttony and its deception. First, we remind ourselves that food is not an end in itself but exists to remind us of our soul's need for Christ. Second, because we enjoy the Lord's Supper with other believers, we renounce all miserly food-grubbing in order to share with one another. The table is a common table, an opportunity to affirm our love for fellow believers (1 Cor. 10:17). Finally, the regulated portions for each individual remind us of the beauty of self-control.[57]

6) *Set aside time for occasional fasting.*

David said of God, "You have put more joy in my heart than they have when their grain and wine abound" (Ps. 4:7). Do you believe God offers you more pleasure than a full belly? Try it and see. You won't be disappointed.[58]

---

56   "The Spiritual Blessings of the Gospel Represented by a Feast," in *Sermons and Discourses: 1723–1729*, ed. Kenneth P. Minkema; vol. 14 of *Works of Jonathan Edwards Online* (New Haven, Conn.: Yale University Press, 1997), 286. Available online at http://edwards.yale.edu/research/browse.

57   At Bethlehem Baptist Church, for example, one of the weekend services offers pre-cut portions of bread to be dipped in a bowl of grape juice. In the other services, people take a small, broken piece of cracker along with a tiny cup of grape juice. Despite the variety in form, both celebrations of the Lord's Supper feature limited portions for each participant.

58   For excellent biblical and practical guidance in the discipline of fasting, see John Piper, *A Hunger for God: Desiring God through Fasting and Prayer*, Redesign ed. (Wheaton, IL: Crossway, 2013).

7) Set aside time for occasional feasting.

I include this counsel right after fasting not because I want to minimize the importance of fasting but because I want to make sure we don't react to our overeating by treating food itself as the problem. Paul said he had "learned the secret of facing plenty and hunger, abundance and need" (Phil. 4:12). Paul knew how to fast; Paul also knew how to feast. He could do both to the glory of God because he saw that both situations required Christian contentment (Phil. 4:11). May we likewise feel such satisfaction in our union with Christ that we can, with equal resolve, skip lunch on Tuesday and go back for seconds at the Sunday potluck.

8) Give thanks before your meal.

Gratitude suffocates gluttony. We are less likely to worship a dish we regard as a gift from the Lord. Praying before meals is no guarantee against gluttony. Like all good habits, it can quickly turn perfunctory. But injecting a holy (and concise!) pause before filling your plate can go a long way to subduing a rebel palate.

9) Memorize Scripture.

If we live by the word of God and not by food alone, then surely a powerful defense against the deceitfulness of gluttony is having our mental refrigerators well-stocked with Scripture. It was by this means that Jesus withstood the temptation to satisfy his hunger unlawfully (Matt. 4:1–4; Luke 4:1–4). For starters, you might try devoting to memory some of the texts we've looked at in this chapter.

10) Stay active.

Idleness is a petri dish for gluttony. How often do we eat simply because we're bored and have nothing better to do? Physical activity, on the other hand, can regulate our cravings and even increase our enjoyment of food. So, in addition to the suggestions above, try going on a walk with your family, playing a game of basketball, or raking the leaves in your backyard. God's gift to us, after all, is not only eating and drinking, but also taking pleasure *in all our toil* (Eccles. 3:13).

Gluttony, as we have seen, is the worship of food. Through Christ, however, God has delivered us from the tyranny of our bellies so that, rather than eat to our own destruction, we can know the joy of eating to the glory of God (1 Cor. 10:31). May the Lord make all grace abound to us so that we might taste and see, again and again, that he is good (Ps. 34:8).

8

Lust

JOHN PIPER

Lust, of course, could be an inordinate desire for other things—for money or food, for power or praise. But since the historic list of deadly sins includes greed, gluttony, pride, and envy, we will treat lust as a sexual sin. So let's begin with a biblical definition. *Lust is a sexual desire that dishonors its object and disregards God.* Let me show you where I see this definition in 1 Thessalonians 4:1–8.

> *Brothers, we ask and urge you in the Lord Jesus, that as you received from us how you ought to walk and to please God, just as you are doing, that you do so more and more. ² For you know what instructions we gave you through the Lord Jesus. ³ For this is the will of God, your sanctification: that you abstain from sexual immorality; ⁴ that each one of you know how to control his own body in holiness and honor, ⁵ not in the passion of lust like the Gentiles who do not know God; ⁶ that no one transgress and wrong his brother in this matter, because the Lord is an avenger in all these things, as we told you beforehand and solemnly warned you. ⁷ For God has not called us for impurity, but in holiness. ⁸ Therefore whoever disregards this, disregards not man but God, who gives his Holy Spirit to you.*

There are various suggested translations of verses 4-5. The
ESV above says, "that each one of you know how to *control
his own body* in holiness and honor, not in the passion of lust
like the Gentiles who do not know God." The RSV says, "that
each one of you know how to *take a wife* for himself in holiness and honor, not in the passion of lust like heathen who
do not know God." The NASB says, most literally, "that each
of you know how to *possess his own vessel* in sanctification and
honor, not in lustful passion, like the Gentiles who do not
know God." The words in italics translate the same phrase
from the original Greek. You can see the reason for the ambi-
guity. The literal "vessel" could refer to the man's own sexual
organs, or the woman's. It is not necessary to resolve this issue
in order to see the meaning of lust that is common to all of
these translations.

LUST DISHONORS ITS OBJECT

Notice that verses 4 and 5 tell us to do something one way,
but not another way. Take a wife or control your body/vessel
"in holiness and honor, *not* in the passion of lust." Note the
contrast: "in holiness and honor, *not* in the passion of lust."
So the passion of lust is the opposite of holiness and honor.
That's where I get my definition for lust.

Sexual desire in itself is good. God made it in the beginning. It has its proper place. But it was made to be governed,
regulated, and guided by two concerns: honor toward the
other person and holiness toward God. Lust is what sexual
desire becomes when that honor and that holiness are miss-
ing.

Take honor, for instance. God established a relationship
called marriage, in which one man and one woman make a
lifelong covenant to honor each other with faithfulness and
love. Sexual desire becomes the servant and the spice of that

covenant bond of mutual honor. Therefore, to say to another person (with or without using words), "I want you to satisfy my sexual desire with you, but I do not want you as a covenant partner in marriage," basically means, "I want to use your body for my pleasure, but I do not want you as a whole person." That is dishonoring, and therefore lustful. Lust is sexual desire minus a commitment to honor the other person.

LUST DISREGARDS GOD

But that's not all. The text says, "in *holiness* and honor, not in the passion of lust." Sexual holiness has to do with God—being set apart for God. So verse 5 reads, "Not in the passion of lust like the Gentiles *who do not know God*." Truly knowing God, and acting like it, keeps sexual desire from becoming lust. Verse 8, "whoever disregards [the call for holiness], disregards not man but God, who gives his Holy Spirit to you." The root issue in lust is regard for God. Holiness is living in supreme regard for a holy God.

Lust is the opposite. Lust is sexual desire that is not regulated or governed or guided by a supreme regard for God. God created sexuality. He created it good and beautiful, for the good of his creatures. He alone has the wisdom and the right to tell us how to use it for his glory and our good. Lust is what that sexual desire becomes when we give it rein and disregard God.

In summary, then, lust is a sexual desire that dishonors its object and disregards God. It is the corruption of a good thing by the absence of honorable commitment and by the absence of a supreme regard for God. If your sexual desire is not guided by respect for the honor of others and regard for the holiness of God, it is lust.

THE DEADLY DANGER OF LUST

Now, why does that matter? Why is lust a big deal? Isn't sexual sin, especially when it's just a desire and not an act, sin with a little *s*? Shouldn't we get on with bigger issues like global pandemics, and human trafficking, and terrorist threats, and vast poverty?

Some say sexual attitudes and sexual behavior are a matter of relatively insignificant personal piety. What counts is whether you fight these massive social and global evils. Sexual promiscuity is simply no big deal if you are standing publicly against racial injustice and sex trafficking. Looking at pornography on the internet is utterly insignificant if you are on your way to a consultation on global warming. This is the mindset of millions.

That is the way the human mind reasons when a supreme regard for God has been forsaken. But that is not what God has said. What is God's estimate of how important your sexual life is? Is it a big deal? Verse 6: ". . . that no one transgress and wrong his brother in this matter, because the *Lord is an avenger in all these things*, as we told you beforehand and solemnly warned you."

This means that the consequences of lust are going to be as bad, or worse, than the consequences of war. All war can do is kill your body. And Jesus said, "Do not fear those who kill the body and after that have no more that they can do. But I will warn you whom to fear. Fear him who after he has killed has power to cast into hell" (Luke 12:4–5). In other words, God's vengeance is much more fearful than earthly annihilation. According to 1 Thessalonians 4:6, God's vengeance is coming upon those who disregard warnings against lust. "The Lord is an avenger in all these things."

LUST AND ETERNAL SECURITY

Some years ago, I spoke to the student body of a Christian high school on the topic, "Ten Lessons for Fighting Lust." Lesson number six was, "Ponder the eternal danger of lust."

My text was Matthew 5:28–29, where Jesus says, "Everyone who looks at a woman with lustful intent has already committed adultery with her in his heart. If your right eye causes you to sin, tear it out and throw it away. For it is better that you lose one of your members than that your whole body be thrown into hell."" I pointed out that Jesus said heaven and hell are at stake in what you do with your eyes, and with your imagination.

After the message, one of the students came up to me and asked, "Are you saying, then, that a person can lose his salvation?" This is exactly the same response I got a few years earlier when I confronted a man about the adultery in which he was living. I patiently tried to understand his situation, and I pled with him to return to his wife. Then I said, "You know, don't you, that Jesus says if you don't fight this sin with the kind of seriousness that is willing to gouge out your own eye, you will go to hell and suffer there forever?" He looked at me in utter disbelief, as though he had never heard anything like this in his life. He said, "You mean you think a person can lose his salvation?"

I have learned again and again from first-hand experience that there are many professing Christians who have a view of salvation that disconnects it from real life. They nullify the warnings of the Bible and put the person who claims to be a Christian, but wages no war against his sin, beyond the reach of biblical threats. Such doctrine is comforting thousands on their way to hell. Jesus said, if you don't fight lust, you won't go to heaven. The stakes are much higher than global terror-

ism. If you don't fight lust, you will not go to heaven (1 Pet.
2:11; Col. 3:6; Gal. 5:21; 1 Cor. 6:10; Heb. 12:14).

JUSTIFYING FAITH IS LUST-FIGHTING FAITH

Are we not, then, saved by faith—by believing in Jesus Christ?
Isn't justification by faith alone? Yes, we are indeed saved by
faith, and justification is by faith alone. Those who persevere
in faith shall be saved (Matt. 24:13; 10:22; 1 Cor. 15:3; Col. 1:23;
2 Thess. 2:13). When God lays hold of us through saving faith,
we are moved to lay hold of him. "I press on to make it my
own, *because* Christ Jesus has made me his own" (Phil. 3:12).
How do you lay hold on eternal life? Paul gives the answer in
1 Timothy 6:12. "Fight the good fight of faith: lay hold on eternal life." We lay hold on eternal life by fighting the good fight
of faith. Saving faith is not a momentary thing. It is the act
of the saved soul every day. And it is a battle, because Satan
wants to destroy it (Luke 22:31–32).

This leads us to our main concern—to show that the
fight against *lust* is a battle against *unbelief*. The fight for sexual purity is the fight of faith. The great error that I am trying
to explode is that faith in God is one thing and the fight for
holiness is another, separate thing—the error that faith gets
you to heaven, and holiness gets you rewards. You get your
justification by faith, and you get the power for your sanctification by works. You start the Christian life in the power of
the Spirit, and you press on in the efforts of the flesh. This is
a serious error. . . . Some have said the battle for obedience is
optional, because only faith is necessary for salvation.

Our response: the battle for obedience is absolutely necessary for salvation because it is, at root, the fight of faith.
The battle against lust is absolutely necessary for salvation
because it is the battle against unbelief. Faith alone delivers

from hell, and the faith that delivers from hell is the faith that delivers from lust.

A GREATER GOSPEL

This gospel is a greater gospel than the other. It's the gospel of God's victory over sin, not just his tolerance of sin. It is the gospel of Romans 6:14: "Sin will have no dominion over you, since you are not under law but under grace." Almighty grace! Sovereign grace!

> *He breaks the power of cancelled sin,*
> *He sets the prisoner free;*
> *His blood can make the foulest clean,*
> *His blood availed for me.*

"Blessed are the pure in heart, for they shall see God" (Matt. 5:8). This is God's demand, and this is God's gift. It is all of grace. That is why the decisive fight against lust is the fight of faith—the fight to daily welcome and treasure Christ so fully that temptation to sin loses its power over us. The battle against lust is the battle against unbelief. The fight of faith is the battle to be satisfied in all that God is for us in Jesus. Lust loses its power to the extent we believe in Christ like this.

YOU CAN KNOW GOD—AND NOT KNOW HIM

In 1 Thessalonians 4:5, Paul says, " . . . not in the passion of lust like the Gentiles who do not know God." Do you see what that implies about the root of lust? Not knowing God is the root cause of lust. Take a wife, or control of your body/vessel, *not* in the passion of lust because that is what people do *who do not know God.*

Paul doesn't mean that mere head knowledge about God overcomes lust. In Mark 1:24, Jesus is about to cast a demon out of a man, when the unclean spirit cries out, "I know who you are, the Holy One of God!" Satan and his hosts have some very accurate *knowledge* about God and Jesus, but that is not the kind of knowledge Paul has in mind here. The knowledge he has in mind is a knowledge of God for the supreme value and beauty that he really is. This kind of knowing is a kind of tasting. "Oh, taste and see that the Lord is good!" (Ps. 34:8). It's the kind of knowledge Paul referred to in 2 Corinthians 4:6—"the light of the *knowledge* of the glory of God in the face of Christ" (see Gal. 4:8; 1 Cor. 2:14; 2 Pet. 1:3–4). It's the soul-recognition of God's greatness and worth and glory and grace and power. It's knowledge that stuns you, and humbles you. It's knowledge that wins you and holds you. It's the kind of knowledge of beauty you don't have when you feel ho-hum during the Hallelujah Chorus, or grumble on the rim of the Grand Canyon. It is possible to hear, and not hear, to see, and not see (Matt. 13:13). That is not the kind of knowledge we need.

True knowledge looks like Lydia's, when the Lord opened the eyes of her heart (Acts 16:14). At one moment you think you will burst with its fullness, and suddenly there is a chasm of longing for more. It's the kind of knowing we call faith—"the assurance of things hoped for, the conviction of things not seen" (Heb. 11:1). It's a knowledge that's so real, so precious, so satisfying to your soul, that any thought, any attitude, any emotion, any addiction which threatens to hinder this knowledge will be attacked with all the spiritual zeal of a threatened life. This is the fight of faith that rages in the godly soul when lust lures the mind away from God.

THE PURE SHALL SEE GOD

I close with an illustration from an article I read years ago, and with a way for preparing to fight. The article was unsigned, but written by a preacher who for ten years was in bondage to lust. He tells the story of what finally released him. It is such a resounding confirmation of what I am trying to say that I want to quote the key paragraph.

He ran across a book by Francois Mauriac called *What I Believe*. In it Mauriac admitted how the plague of guilt had not freed him from lust. He concludes that there is one powerful reason to seek purity, the one Christ gives in the Beatitudes: "Blessed are the pure in heart, for they shall see God." The unnamed pastor writes,

> *The thought hit me like a bell rung in a dark, silent hall. So far, none of the scary, negative arguments against lust had succeeded in keeping me from it .... But here was a description of what I was missing by continuing to harbor lust: I was limiting my own intimacy with God. The love he offers is so transcendent and possessing that it requires our faculties to be purified and cleansed before we can possibly contain it. Could he, in fact, substitute another thirst and another hunger for the one I had never filled? Would Living Water somehow quench lust? That was the gamble of faith.*[59]

It was not a gamble. You can't lose when you turn to God. He discovered this in his own life, and the lesson he learned is absolutely right: The way to fight lust is to feed faith with the knowledge of an irresistibly glorious God.

ANTHEM: A STRATEGY FOR FIGHTING LUST

Here's the strategy I have used countless times myself in battling the unbelief of lust. With these six steps, I have in mind men *and* women. For men, the crisis is more obvious. The need for warfare against the bombardment of visual temptation to fixate on sexual images is urgent. For women, it is often less obvious, but just as great, especially if we broaden the scope of temptation to food or figure or relational fantasies. What I am focusing on here is the realm of thought, imagination, and desire that leads to sexual misconduct. So here is one set of strategies in the war against wrong desires. I put it in the form of an acronym, ANTHEM.

A—*Avoid*

Avoid, as much as possible and reasonable, the sights and situations that arouse unfitting desire. I say "possible and reasonable" because some exposure to temptation is inevitable. And I say "unfitting desire" because not all desires for sex, food, and family are bad. We know when the desires are unfitting, unhelpful, and moving toward becoming enslaving. We know our weaknesses and what triggers them. "Avoiding" is a biblical strategy. "Flee youthful passions and pursue righteousness" (2 Tim. 2:22). "Make no provision for the flesh, to gratify its desires" (Rom. 13:14). And, of course, this is done out of faith. That is, it is done because we have a superior satisfaction in Christ over all things and we do not want to tempt our fickle hearts beyond what is necessary.

N—*No*

Say *no* to every lustful thought right away. And say it boldly with the authority of Jesus Christ. "In the name of Jesus, *No!*"

You don't have much more than a few seconds. Give the lust-ful thought more unopposed time than that, and it will lodge itself with such force as to be almost immovable. Say it out loud, if you dare. Be tough and warlike. As John Owen said, "Be killing sin or it will be killing you." Strike fast and strike hard. "Resist the devil, and he will flee from you" (James 4:7).

T—Turn

Turn the mind forcefully toward Christ as a superior satisfac-tion. Saying "no" will not suffice. You must move from defense to offense. Fight fire with fire. Attack the inferior promises of sin with the superior promises of Christ. The Bible calls lusts "deceitful desires" (Eph. 4:22). They lie. They promise more than they can deliver. The Bible calls them "passions of your former *ignorance*" (1 Pet. 1:14). Only fools yield. "All at once he follows her, as an ox goes to the slaughter" (Prov. 7:22). De-ceit is defeated by truth. Ignorance is defeated by knowledge. It must be glorious truth and beautiful knowledge. We must stock our minds with the superior promises and pleasures of Jesus. Then we must turn to them immediately after saying, "No!"

H—Hold

Hold the promise and the pleasure of Christ firmly in your mind until it pushes the other images out. "Fix your eyes on Jesus" (Heb. 12:2). Here is where many fail. They give in too quickly. They say, "I tried to push it out, and it didn't work." I ask, "How long did you try?" A minute? Five? Ten? How long did you make war on this one temptation? How hard did you exert your mind? The mind is a muscle. You can flex it with vehemence. Take the kingdom violently (Matt. 11:12). Be brutal. Hold the promise of Christ before your eyes. Hold it.

Hold it! Don't let it go! Keep holding it! How long? As long as it takes. Fight! For Christ's sake, fight until you win. If an electric garage door were about to crush your child you would hold it up with all your might and holler for help, and hold it and hold it and hold it and hold it. Until it cut your fingers off.

E—Enjoy

Enjoy a superior satisfaction. Cultivate capacities for pleasure in Christ. One reason lust reigns in so many is that Christ has so little appeal. We default to deceit because we have little delight in Christ. Don't say, "That kind of delighting just isn't me." What steps have you taken to waken affection for Jesus? Have you fought for joy? Don't be fatalistic. You were created to treasure Christ with all your heart—more than you treasure sex or sugar or sports or shopping. If you have little taste for Jesus, competing pleasures will triumph. Plead with God for the satisfaction you don't have: "Satisfy us in the morning with your steadfast love, that we may rejoice and be glad all our days" (Ps. 90:14). Then look, and look, and look at the most magnificent Person in the universe until you see him as supremely magnificent and satisfying as he really is.

M—Move

Move into a useful activity away from idleness and other vulnerable behaviors. Lust grows fast in the garden of leisure. Find good work to do, and do it with all your might. "Do not be slothful in zeal, be fervent in spirit, serve the Lord" (Rom. 12:11). "Be steadfast, immovable, always *abounding* in the work of the Lord" (1 Cor. 15:58). Abound in work. Get up and do something. Sweep a room. Hammer a nail. Write a letter. Fix a faucet. And do it for Jesus's sake. You were made to manage and create. Christ died to make you "zealous for good works"

(Titus 2:14). Displace deceitful lusts with a passion for good deeds.

And in between the moments of hand-to-hand combat with lustful thoughts, devote yourself in every way to seeing and savoring the superior worth of Christ. This will be the victory. "I count everything as loss because of the surpassing worth of knowing Christ Jesus my Lord" (Phil. 3:8).

❈ desiringGod

Everyone wants to be happy. Our website was born and built for happiness. We want people everywhere to understand and embrace the truth that God is most glorified in us when we are most satisfied in him. We've collected more than thirty years of John Piper's speaking and writing, including translations into more than forty languages. We also provide a daily stream of new written, audio, and video resources to help you find truth, purpose, and satisfaction that never end. And it's all available free of charge, thanks to the generosity of people who've been blessed by the ministry.

If you want more resources for true happiness, or if you want to learn more about our work at Desiring God, we invite you to visit us at www.desiringGod.org.

www.desiringGod.org

Made in the USA
Charleston, SC
25 January 2015